KEY
WOMEN
WRITERS
EDITOR SUE ROE

DOROTHY
RICHARDSON

D1628171

KEY
WOMEN
WRITERS
EDITOR: SUE ROE

DOROTHY RICHARDSON

JEAN RADFORD

Senior Lecturer in English Literature
Hatfield Polytechnic

HARVESTER WHEATSHEAF

New York London Toronto Sydney Tokyo
Singapore

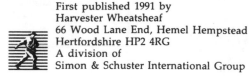

First published 1991 by
Harvester Wheatsheaf
66 Wood Lane End, Hemel Hempstead
Hertfordshire HP2 4RG
A division of
Simon & Schuster International Group

Typeset in 10/12 pt Palatino
by Photo·graphics, Honiton, Devon

Printed and bound in Great Britain by
Billing and Sons Ltd, Worcester

British Library Cataloguing in Publication Data

Radford, Jean
  Dorothy Richardson. – (Key women writers series)
  I. Title   II. Series
  823 .

  ISBN 0–7108–1052–0 (cloth)
  ISBN 0–7108–1070–9

---

1 2 3 4 5   95 94 93 92 91

To
L. J. and E,
'this time with a little dedication'

Titles in the Key Women Writers Series

Gillian Beer	*George Eliot*
Paula Bennett	*Emily Dickinson*
Penny Boumelha	*Charlotte Brontë*
Stevie Davies	*Emily Brontë*
Rachel Blau DuPlessis	*H.D.*
Kate Fullbrook	*Katherine Mansfield*
Jane Heath	*Simone de Beauvoir*
Coral Ann Howells	*Jean Rhys*
Deborah Johnson	*Iris Murdoch*
Angela Leighton	*Elizabeth Barrett Browning*
Jean Radford	*Dorothy Richardson*
Susan Sheridan	*Christina Stead*
Patsy Stoneman	*Elizabeth Gaskell*
Nicole Ward Jouve	*Colette*

Key Women Writers

The *Key Women Writers* series has developed in a spirit of challenge, exploration and interrogation. Looking again at the work of women writers with established places in the mainstream of the literary tradition, the series asks, in what way can such writers be regarded as feminist? Does their status as canonical writers ignore the notion that there are ways of writing and thinking which are specific to women? Or is it the case that such writers have integrated within their writing a feminist perspective which so subtly maintains its place that these are writers who have, hitherto, been largely misread?

In answering these questions, each volume in the series is attentive to aspects of composition such as style and voice, as well as to the ideas and issues to emerge out of women's writing practice. For while recent developments in literary and feminist theory have played a significant part in the creation of the series, feminist theory represents no specific methodology, but rather an opportunity to broaden our range of responses to the issues of history, psychology and gender which have always engaged women writers. A new and creative dynamics between a woman critic and her female subject has been made possible by recent developments in feminist theory, and the series seeks to reflect the important critical insights which have emerged out of this new, essentially feminist, style of engagement.

It is not always the case that literary theory can be directly transposed from its sources in other disciplines to the practice of reading writing by women. The series investigates the possibility that a distinction may need to be made between feminist politics and the literary criticism of women's writing which has not, up to now, been sufficiently emphasised. Feminist reading, as well as feminist writing, still needs to be constantly interpreted and reinterpreted. The complexity and range of choice implicit in this procedure are represented throughout the series. As works of criticism, all the volumes in the series represent wide-ranging and creative styles of discourse, seeking at all times to express the particular resonances and perspectives of individual women writers.

Sue Roe

Contents

Acknowledgements and Abbreviations xiii

Introduction 1

1. Reading (in) *Pilgrimage* 6

2. A form of quest 25

3. London: space for a woman 44

4. The enigma of woman 66

5. Looking back (at the mother) 86

6. The subject of writing: *écriture féminine* 106

Postscript 134

Notes 139
Selected bibliography 146
Index 155

Acknowledgements

My thanks, first of all, to those scholars and critics whose work on Dorothy Richardson has informed and stimulated my own – particularly Rachel Blau DuPlessis, Gloria Fromm, Gillian Hanscombe and Shirley Rose. Thanks also to friends and colleagues who have read and made comments on chapters as these appeared, Dennis Brown, Rosalind Delmar, and Alison Light; to my students on the MA in Literature course at Hatfield Polytechnic, who encouraged me with their interest and ideas; to Hatfield Polytechnic for 6 months sabbatical leave in 1989 and the loan of a word-processor; and lastly thanks to all those who have helped by looking after my children so that I could write this book.

Abbreviations

All references to *Pilgrimage* are to the 1979 Virago edition. After quotations the numbers in brackets, e.g. (I, 47), indicate the volume and page number in this edition.

Note

Richardson's syntax and punctuation are unusual, in particular she frequently uses ellipses or stops to indicate gaps or interruptions in the heroine's consciousness. All such stops appearing in quotations belong to the text, unless they are in parentheses, in which case they are my own and signal an omission of part of the text.

Introduction

In a popular detective story of 1928, the detective enters the room of a murder suspect and scans her bookshelves for indications of guilt and innocence:

> Dorothy Richardson – Virginia Woolf – E.B.C. Jones – May Sinclair – Katherine Mansfield – the modern female writers are well represented aren't they?[1]

For Lord Peter Wimsey, the detective, the names of these modern female writers provide a clue to the character of the accused and, indirectly, put him on the track of the real criminal. But in this story the modern woman with her suspect sexuality turns out to be innocent and the murderer is her ex-lover and a man from the Bellona Club. For me, an avid reader of Dorothy Sayers, this reference was my first introduction to the name of Dorothy Richardson, although it was not until some time later that I hunted down the sequence of novels entitled *Pilgrimage*.

Pilgrimage, I discovered, consists of thirteen different novels, twelve of which were published between 1915 and 1938 and the thirteenth and last appeared in the posthumous edition of 1967. It traces the life of Miriam Henderson, a middle-class English girl, in the years between 1891 and 1912, through the consciousness of the heroine. The details are modelled on Dorothy Richardson's own life and almost all the narrative events and characters correspond to those in her life history: the father's bankruptcy, the time in Germany as a governess, clerical life in London during the scandals of the New Woman

1

and the trial of Oscar Wilde, friendships with Fabians and feminists and explorations into religion and philosophy. If Doris Lessing's *The Golden Notebook* can be compared to a capacious cupboard in which the reader rummages at will,[2] *Pilgrimage* is more like an enormous room, crammed with portraits and memories, with light and dark places, scents and textures, dusty cretonne at the window – but with the window always open to the streets of London.

In Sayers' lifetime, after the First World War and during the 1920s and 1930s, Dorothy Richardson was well known as one of 'the modern female writers' and her name was constantly linked with those of Woolf and Mansfield and often, as here, given precedence. During these years, among women writers as diverse as Dorothy L. Sayers and Winifred Bryher, she seems to have been something of a cult figure. Her name was also linked, though in a more subordinate role, with those of Joyce and Proust, as one of a group of writers renowned for their experiments in narrative form. This early recognition and interest faded however, and although Richardson continued writing well into her eighties, 'abominably unknown' as Ford Madox Ford put it, she died in poverty and obscurity. Shortly before her death in 1957 in a south London nursing home, the matron reported to a visitor that Richardson suffered from delusions, one of which was that she thought she was a writer. 'But she *is* a writer', her visitor insisted.[3]

Ironically, it was only with death that the reputation of her life's work *Pilgrimage*, began to revive. As Leon Edel, Henry James's biographer, wrote in his obituary essay:

> Few writers have placed so double-weighted a burden upon their readers. And yet if the challenge is met and the empathy achieved, Dorothy Richardson offers us on certain pages, a remarkable emotional luminescence – as well as, historically speaking, a record of the trying out of a new technique, the opportunity to examine a turning point in the modern English novel. There is a distinct possibility that a new generation of readers – if there continue to be readers at all – may truly discover Dorothy Richardson for the first time.[4]

That time, I think, has now come. The revision of the 'modernist' canon (Joyce, Pound and Eliot with Woolf as the token woman) opens up new possibilities for reading and a

new set of historical circumstances has created a new generation
of readers. For the women's movement of the 1970s and 1980s
has produced not merely the lost and forgotten texts of the
earlier period, but a new audience with the 'empathy' to take
up the challenge that Richardson offers. Since the full length
biography was published in 1977 and the new four-volume
edition of *Pilgrimage* in 1979, this seems a good time for a rereading of Woolf's sister-writer. The opportunity to enjoy
Pilgrimage's 'emotional luminescence' is also, for us, an opportunity to take up the 'burden' of an earlier generation's sense
of itself: their consciousness of what it meant to be a woman
during the transition from a Victorian to a modern world.
Whether one reads *Pilgrimage* as experimental fiction, spiritual
autobiography, case-history, or documentary, its concern with
sexual difference at the beginning of the century makes it of
enormous interest to readers – men and women – at the end
of the twentieth century.

The method of *Pilgrimage*, which in 1957 seemed to impose
such burdens on its readers, is now part of its fascination.
Developments in televisual narratives and narrative theory,
and, since the advent of postmodernism, an increased interest
in the movement called modernism, have each opened up new
ways of reading. In the context of feminist theories of *écriture
féminine*, the new techniques employed in the novel make a
fresh and different kind of sense. Richardson's style – her
deviations from the standard syntactical forms – takes on a
special significance. Virginia Woolf in her review of *Revolving
Lights* (1923), the seventh novel in the sequence, was one of
the first to comment on this style:

> She has invented, or, if she has not invented, developed and
> applied to her own uses, a sentence which we might call the
> psychological sentence of the feminine gender. It is of a more
> elastic fibre than the old, capable of stretching to the extreme,
> of suspending the frailest particles, of enveloping the vaguest
> shapes. . . . It is a woman's sentence, but only in the sense that it
> is used to describe a woman's mind by a writer who is neither
> proud nor afraid of anything that she may discover in the
> psychology of her sex.[5]

The length and elasticity of Richardson's sentences are
matched by the length – over 2000 pages – of *Pilgrimage* and

this is frequently attacked by its critics. The body of the text, it is said, is too big, too bulky to be good canon fodder: a loose baggy monster, it exasperates its readers and critics by its excessive length, its shapelessness, its narcissism. 'Feminine without the charm' Lionel Trilling called it. It goes on and on, pleonastic, plotless, like some interminable analysis which refuses to come to an end. The thirteenth novel, *March Moonlight* is indeed an unfinished unrevised draft which Dent included in the posthumous 1967 edition. Only Richardson's death (and her publishers) brought it to a close.

Yet, if the challenge is met and one is not looking for finalities, the length of the text can prove a source of *active* pleasure, for what one enjoys is the activity of reading, not the satisfaction of coming to an end. As Roland Barthes argues in his essay 'From work to text', writing and reading, like playing and listening to music, were once scarcely differentiated activities; if one could read or listen, one could also write or play, since these activities were usually the privilege of a particular class. The two roles then separated out, the bourgeois public delegated its 'playing' and 'writing' to professionals, themselves becoming passive consumers of the performance or product. The 'text', Barthes claims, is that kind of writing which does not allow its reader to consume it, but asks for the practical collaboration of the reader. *Pilgrimage*, in my view, is this kind of 'text', it demands that the reader become a co-author, interpreting or 'playing' the words on the page as if they were a musical score. Without the 'practical collaboration' and skills of the reader, the 'text' remains inert. In Barthes' words:

> The reduction of reading to a consumption is clearly responsible for the 'boredom' experienced by many in the face of the modern ('unreadable') text, the avant-garde film or painting: to be bored means that one cannot produce the text, open it out, *set it going*.[6]

My aim, in a series of interpretive readings of *Pilgrimage*, is precisely to open it out, to *set it going*, so that other readers may be stimulated, or provoked, to produce their own readings. *Pilgrimage* marks the passage of women from objects of another's discourse to women as subjects of their own; it articulates a new consciousness in a form designed to transform the consciousness of its readers. For one of Richardson's most important, and most feminist, points is that if writing and reading help to shape the way we live, or at least shape the meanings by which we live, it is vital that the reader should play an active and collaborative role in the process.

Chapter One

Reading (in) Pilgrimage

Why is Luther like a dyspeptic blackbird? Because the Diet of Worms did not agree with him. (I, 169)

Jokes are rare in *Pilgrimage,* and although there are many riddles this one stands out because it is one of the few with an answer. The schoolgirl joke, recalled by Miriam at a moment of crisis in Germany, depends on a pun, on the point that a signifier may have more than one signified: that 'diet' is an Assembly or Parliament and a planned selection of food; that 'Worms' is a German town on the Rhine and an elongate invertebrate found in the garden; that the verb 'to agree' (from the Latin *ad gratum* – pleasing to) has a double meaning, intellectual as well as digestive. As Freud says in *Jokes and their Relation to the Unconscious,* double meanings are 'the most fertile sources for the techniques of jokes', and as he also points out the purpose of jokes is to yield a pleasure which might not otherwise be available.[1]

This joke in the first novel of *Pilgrimage* makes a point about language and pleasure – typical of Richardson's writing – which is minutely attentive to the tricks that language plays on both the writer and the reader. The riddle of Luther's relationship with the blackbird is based on a trick, on a metaphor where the resemblance is based on language, not on the qualities of the items compared. As such it serves as a playful reminder to the reader about the power of language to shape the world. But the reference to Luther has another, historical, significance for the question of reading. For it was after Luther was cross-examined and imprisoned by the Diet of Worms in 1521, that he began his translation of the Bible into German, and scripture became a driving force in the Reformation. Believing that the Bible would be clear to those who read with faith, he argued that the text should be accessible for all to read (or hear spoken) in their own language. However, his belief that for the faithful scripture could have but one meaning, raised all the problems predicted by the papal authorities. For 'the peasants were to read the book of hope very differently from the princes and from Luther himself'.[2] The schisms of the Holy Roman and Apostolic Church, one might say, also begin with the Word.

Richardson's interest in matters of language and her linguistic skills are described in 'Data for a Spanish publisher', one of her rare autobiographical sketches. Her pleasure in language, she claims there, was established early, in school:

> Even so, there was still the fascination of words, of their sturdy roots, their growth and transformation, and the strange drama of the pouring in from every quarter of the globe of alien words assimilated and modified to the rhythm of our own speech, enriching its poetry and making its spelling and its pronunciation the joy of those who love it and the despair of all others. (Richardson, 1989: 155)

After describing her reading during the London years, Richardson recounts her entry into writing:

> Meanwhile I had begun to write. Translations and freelance journalism had promised release from routine work that could not engage the essential forces of my being. The small writing-table in my attic became the centre of my life. (Richardson, 1989: 139)

Coming to writing late in life, like George Eliot, Richardson began by writing reviews and translations. The first volume of *Pilgrimage (Pointed Roofs)* was not published until 1915, when she was 42. However, her theories about writing were developed earlier from her work as a reader and reviewer and can be traced from her review of Whitman in 1906 through to the 1939 review of Joyce's *Finnegan's Wake*.[3] Repeatedly, Richardson stresses the importance of language as a *common* medium between writer and reader:

the writer, whatever his struggles, is handling a medium he has used from infancy onwards and whose arduous acquisitions and final mastery he has long since forgotten. It lies, ready for use, stored up within him in fragments each of which is a living unit complete in form and significance. Within this medium the reader is also at home. (Richardson, 1930: 12)

She was sceptical about the special status accorded to the writer. 'Readers', she asserted, 'are far too modest. Always they regard themselves as recipients, never as donors.'[4] For Richardson reading is a creative art and reading and writing are complementary and analogous acts:

while subject to the influence of a work of art, we are ourselves artists, supplying creative collaboration in the form of a reaction of the totality of our creative and constructive and disinterested being.[5]

A story of reading

The question of reading figures largely in *Pilgrimage*. It is, first of all, Miriam Henderson's apprenticeship to the craft of writing. If Proust's twelve-volume novel *A la recherche du temps perdu* can be summed up as 'Marcel becomes a writer', equally the thirteen novels of *Pilgrimage* could be summarised as 'Miriam becomes a writer'. Her pilgrimage towards this goal takes her through years of reading, through all the highways and byways of late Victorian textuality to the statement in the last volume, *March Moonlight:* 'While I write, everything vanishes but what I contemplate' (IV. 657) which signals her accession to the role of writer. *Pilgrimage* is an epic which is also a *Künstlerroman*, the story of an artist in the making, but only after serving her time in the study of the craft (reading), can she proceed to the practice of it (writing).

What that reading consists of is very clearly signalled in the names and italicised titles contained in the text; these operate as signposts to Miriam's discursive journey: from *Villette* in *Pointed Roofs*, through Ouida in *Backwater*, on to Darwin, Geddes and Schenk in *The Tunnel*, then to the Fabian pamphlets and the titles from science, religion and philosophy in the subsequent volumes before reaching the contemporary fiction of Conrad and James. And what she learns from these masters is that 'The indirect method's the method. Old Conrad' (III, 353). But she also learns that writing, like reading, depends on one's gender position.

If most of what Miriam reads in the years between 1891 and 1912 disagrees with her, this is chiefly because she discovers the problems of reading as a woman. From the poetry, fairy-tales and textbooks of her childhood, she turns in adolescence to the romantic fiction of Mrs Hungerford, Rosa Nouchette Carey and Ouida, borrowed from a Circulating Library for a weekly subscription of 2d (I, 281). In this guilty midnight reading she finds a mirror for her secret hopes and fears, but after 'losing herself' in these books, she begins to find herself in a strange position, identifying not with the heroine but with the anti-heroine:

> If Rosa Nouchette Carey knew me, she'd make me one of the bad characters who are turned out of happy homes. I'm some sort of bad unsimple woman. O damn, damn. (I, 284)

Looking for herself within the text, she is confronted with an image of 'woman' and a series of complex recognitions:

> The mere sitting with the text held before her eyes gave her the feeling of being strongly confronted. (I, 286)

Taking the question of 'woman' from romance to science, Miriam discovers with rage and disbelief, that her problems with sexual identity are not peculiar to herself but that the whole of womanhood has a problem:

> *inferior*, mentally morally, intellectually and physically. . .her development arrested in the interests of special functions. . .reverting later toward the male type. . . . Woman is undeveloped man. . . If one could die of the loathsome visions. . . I must die. . . I can't go on living in it. . .the whole world full of *creatures*, half-human. And I am one of the half-human ones, or shall be, if I don't stop now. (II, 220)

Her reading of evolutionary theories is traumatic. In the pre-Freudian theories of the Social Darwinians, women, it seems, are not merely 'castrated' but not fully human. The blow to the protagonist's narcissism is presented around a series of readings, in encyclopedias, the *British Medical Journal* and the works of Thomas Henry Huxley to the point where she decides that 'All books were poisoned. . . . All life was poisoned, for women, at the very essence' (II, 220).

> Dyspepsia: Difficulty or derangement of digestion: indigestion: applied esp. to disorder of the stomach, usually involving weakness, loss of appetite, and depression of the spirits.
>
> (*Oxford English Dictionary*)

Richardson's heroine loses, temporarily, much of her appetite for books and enters into a depression of spirits – a veritable slough of despond – which is traced through *The Tunnel* and subsequent volumes. The effects of this reading are presented in some detail. She takes refuge from her depression in anger with the male writers, but also with the women who share her fate as 'undeveloped man'. In terms of the Luther joke Miriam, the daughter of a Darwinian, is 'dyspeptic' because she cannot stomach the role given to women in the new stories of evolution. (In a later novel a friend actually calls her 'dyspeptic' (IV, 330).) The disorder is caused by the paternal diet, but it is also linked back to her disgust with the maternal offering in a scene in which she refuses to drink milk and pours it away on 'the filth-sodden earth' (I, 133). Her reaction to the narratives of Huxley, Spencer, Geddes and Maudsley and the Social Darwinians is typical of the intellectual women of her generation: '*How* could Newnham and Girton women endure it' (II, 219)? Women's progenerative role seems to leave no space for individuality.[6]

Miriam's problem at this point is not so much the lack of the phallus, as a lack of a theory of reading which would allow her to challenge the authority of what she reads. She is still one of Luther's 'faithful' readers but

> Religion in the world had nothing but insults for women (. . .) it was the same story everywhere. Even if religion could answer science and prove it wrong there was no hope, for women. No intelligent person can prove science wrong. (II, 222)

Having grasped the point that 'the Bible is not true; it is a culture' (II, 99), Miriam falls victim to the new scientific discourse which consigns women to inferiority with even greater authority. Although suspicious of these scientific texts, she cannot formulate her objections – except by inverting their claims: claiming, for example, that it is women who are fully 'human' and men, by comparison, who are deficient.[7] This reaction, the text suggests, is the mirror image of what it opposes, locking her more firmly into an oppositional structure of Man/Woman.

Reading *Villette* aloud to a woman friend in *The Tunnel* (1919) Miriam tries to characterise the differences between men and women's reading:

> A man's reading was not reading; not a looking and a listening so that things came into the room. It was always an assertion of himself. Men read in loud harsh unnatural voices, in sentences, or in voices that were a commentary on the text, as if they were telling you what to think. . .they preferred reading to being read to; they read as if they were the authors of the text. (II, 261)

The male reader, she feels, assumes a position of authority in relation to language, even when, as here, the text is written by a woman. The irony of this point, which is not lost upon Miriam, is that she too prefers reading to being read to, that she can and does assume a masculine reading position 'She felt that in some way she was like a man reading to a woman' (II, 261). In this passsage and in others like it, Miriam begins to recognise the convoluted relationship between reading and gender, the point that reading as a man or woman may not depend solely on biology, but on a more complex set of factors.

Deadlock (1921) relates Miriam's suspicion that she is not going to agree with Michael Shatov (and everybody else) that *Anna Karenina* is a 'most masterly study of a certain type of woman' (III, 61). Miriam as a reader now appears to know that the *Anna Karenina* she reads will be different from the one that Shatov reads or that Tolstoy wrote. Tolstoy has become a 'scriptor' in Barthes' sense, the originator of the text but not of its meaning. She is free to construct her own reading of Tolstoy's narrative, since as she argues, it is 'the story of a woman told by a man with a man's ideas about people' (III, 59).[8] The realisation does not however resolve her problems with gender and reading, problems which are again staged in *The Trap* (1925), around her reading of Henry James's *The Ambassadors*.

On first reading *The Ambassadors*, Miriam experiences a profound pleasure at the way in which 'he conveyed information without coming forward to announce it' (III, 409). She finds the technique of presentation, the indirect method, both exciting and satisfying. Rereading it for the presentation of Maria Gostrey, however, she becomes aware of a disappointment, and a resistance:

> She now for the first time imagined men reading the magic pages, suffering unconsciously the insidious corruption. This man was a monstrous unilluminated pride. And joy in him was a mark of the same corruption. Pride in discovering the secrets of his technique. Pride in watching it labour with the development of the story. The deep attention demanded by this new way of statement was in itself a self-indulgence. Thought of as enjoyed in a world that held Church Army men it was plain wickedness. (III, 409)

She here identifies her first reading as that of a man, and vehemently repudiates it – as formalist, concerned only with technique, not its meaning in a world containing 'Church Army men'. Miriam learns to read as a woman not, the text suggests, because biologically she *is* a woman, but by imagining the difference between the ways in which a man and a woman might read.

The pleasures of the text are not independent of sexual position since the hypothesis of a male reader changes Miriam's apprehension of a given text; it also changes her position as a reader. The 'masculine' position from which she initially reads is rejected, projected onto a caricature of the male writer/reader and their 'monstrous unilluminated pride'. She begins to read as a woman, not because she is repeating an identity or experience that is given (natural) but by constructing a role in which *she is reading as a woman*. That role is constructed in relation to her identity as a woman, but that too is a construct, and one which is made only in relation to the construction of 'man' at a given period. This passage marks a crucial stage in Miriam's progress as a reader, it proposes a *differential definition* of the woman reader which anticipates many of the recent debates in feminist theories of reading:

> to read as a woman is to avoid reading as a man, to identify the specific defences and distortions of male readings and provide correctives.[9]

The collaborative reader

In the story of Miriam's reading, reading is not just a pleasure but, as she says to a young clergyman, a 'quest': 'Your reading is a habit, like most men's reading, not a quest' (II, 279). In the early novel-chapters of *Pilgrimage*, the quest is a search for knowledge, revelation, for nothing less than 'truth' and like Bunyan's pilgrim she sets out on her voyage of discovery book in hand. She assumes that in some text or other she will find a key to the secrets of the self and universe; the text is supposed to know what she, Miriam, wants (to know). However, once installed in a room of her own, on the seedier side of Bloomsbury, her search takes a rather different direction. The following passage from *The Tunnel* marks a critical re-orientation in Miriam's textual pilgrimage:

> The gaslight glared beautifully over her shoulder down on to the page. . .
>
> *All* that has been said and known in the world is in *language*, in words; all that we know of Christ is in Jewish words; all the dogmas of religion are words; the meaning of words change with people's thoughts. Then no-one *knows* anything for certain. Everything depends on the way a thing is put, and that is a question of some particular civilisation (. . .) So the Bible is not true; it is a culture. (II, 99)

Until this point, Miriam has been using the text as a 'mirror', looking into it to discover the truth about herself and the world. Here she looks again, and what she recognises is not an image of self or a reflection of the world, but *the mirror and its frame*: 'language' and 'words'. Having looked *through* the words in her search for the beyond, she now begins to look *at* the words, the medium itself. Realising for the first time here that there may be no truth, no reality which is not framed in the discourse of 'some particular civilisation', her quest shifts from an absolute to a relative one and she becomes a modern pilgrim . The recognition of the materiality of language brings about an epistemological shift.

In another journey–novel of the period, Molly Bloom also has problems with her reading, with the meaning of words like 'metempsychosis' but the hermeneutic quest falls to another. Joyce positions his woman character 'at home', a

supine Penelope who weaves her discursive web from the
bedroom, beneath a picture of the nymph Calypso where she
lies awaiting the return of the wandering Jew and the prodigal
son. In *Ulysses*, as Marilyn French points out,[10] it is the reader
who makes the journey through Joyce's seas of prose, who
adventures through the rocks and whirlpools of allusion and
pun, who is forced to change tack as the narrative technique
transmutes from one form to another. But when that newly-
born modernist reader, like Leopold Bloom himself, finally
comes home to roost, s/he comes back to Molly Bloom. 'The
one stable self which is always located "at home" and whose
presence is necessary to patriarchy is that of the woman.'[11]

Dorothy Richardson moves her heroine out of the home onto
the streets, out on the city and abroad. Like Joyce, she takes
her reader away from the familiar positions offered in the
nineteenth-century novel. For Richardson refuses to act as
courier, guide or hostess on this excursion; the narrative
technique leaves the reader with few directives as how to read.
Miriam Henderson may be as arrogant as Emma Woodhouse,
as libidinous as Jane Eyre, as ambitious as Dorothea Brooke,
but there is no narrator's voice telling the reader what to
admire or deplore. The writer, the one 'who is supposed to
know' is not telling. So the reader is forced to make her print-
bound journey, as it were, alone with Miriam – or not at all.
Instead of being a passive recipient, the reader is asked to
contribute what Richardson called 'creative collaboration'. It is
this demand on the reader and the reading-process, rather
than the use of 'stream-of-consciousness', which links her
work to that of Joyce and Woolf.

Richardson alludes to both these writers in the Foreword to
the 1938 edition of *Pilgrimage*. Beginning to write, she says,
was like being on a 'fresh pathway, an adventure':

> The lonely track, meanwhile had turned out to be a populous
> highway. Amongst those who had simultaneously entered it, two
> figures stood out. One a woman mounted upon a magnificently
> caparisoned charger, the other a man walking, with eyes devoutly
> closed, weaving as he went a rich garment of new words wherewith
> to clothe the antique dark material of his engrossment.
> News came from France of one Marcel Proust. . . . (I, 10)

The sense of writing as an 'adventure' appears in an earlier statement in which Richardson discusses her theory of art and human consciousness:

> The process may go forward in the form of a conducted tour, the author leading, visible and audible, all the time. Or the material to be contemplated may be thrown upon a screen, the author out of sight and hearing; present, if we seek him, only in attitude toward reality. . .by his accent. . .by his use of adjective, epithet and metaphor. But whatever the means by which the reader's collaboration is secured, a literary work, for reader and writer alike, remains essentially an adventure of the stable contemplative human consciousness. (In Kunitz, 1933: p. 562)

What is noticeable here, apart from the cinematic allusion to the text as 'a screen', is the conception of reading and writing as an *adventure* shared by both writer and reader. There is a levelling of the status of writer and reader. The text is no longer a medium of communication (a message passed from writer to reader); the author relinquishes authority, no longer a conductor/leader but a fellow adventurer. The effects of this conception on Richardson's writing practice, as I shall argue later, are numerous and complex, but it marks Richardson's intention to produce a 'writerly' text.[12]

In *Pilgrimage* the evolution of this method is staged as part of the story of Miriam's reading. It is also presented as part of Miriam's reaction to paternal authority. Pondering over the word 'sivvle' ('Civil') in *Pointed Roofs*, she thinks:

> She would ask Pater before he went. . . No, she would not. If only he would answer a question simply, and not with a superior air as if he had invented the thing he was telling about. (I, 31)

Like the male reader reading aloud, Mr Henderson seems to 'authorise' the information he relates. He cannot assume a neutral position ('out of sight and hearing') which would enable them both to look at the material together on grounds of equality. Miriam's dislike of the authoritative mode, in teaching and in religious services ('these men's sermons') identifies this practice as generally masculine, but her objections crystallise around the figure of her father. In *Honeycomb* she overhears her parents talking:

> Of course they talked in their room. They had talked all their lives; an endless conversation; he laying down the law. . .no end to it. . .the movement of his beard as he spoke, the red lips shining through the fair moustache. (I, 460)

Her search, first as a teacher, then as a writer, is for an alternative, which would position speaker and listener, writer and reader, 'side by side' (I, 333). It is an attempt to avoid 'laying down the law' like her father, but also perhaps, in a Lacanian sense, to evade the law which her father represents.

One of these laws, for Miriam, is the opposition between analytic and synthetic activity, between critical and creative writing. In *Revolving Lights* (1923), talking of Miriam's reviewing activities, Hypo Wilson tells her: 'You're not creative. You've got a good sound mind, a good style, and a curious critical perception. You'll be a critic' (III, 369–70).

In a typically deferred response, Miriam as she begins writing the novel which is in effect *Pilgrimage*, muses:

> What is called 'creation' imaginative transformation, fantasy, invention, is only based on reality (. . .) Can anything produced by man be called 'creation'? The incense burners do not seem to know that in acclaiming what they call 'a work of genius' they are recognising what is potentially within themselves. If it were not, they would not recognise it. (IV, 657)

This is not just a democratic gesture towards the reader (who has managed to reach page 657 of the fourth volume!) but a fundamental part of her writing.

Richardson's deliberate refusal to impose an authorised meaning on *Pilgrimage* imposes a complex burden on her reader. All traces of the authoritative author have been eliminated, and the anonymous narrator not only refuses 'to lay down the law' but offers little in the way of guidance. In the late twentieth century, this practice is now a familiar one and few readers expect a 'conducted tour' in the manner of the 'grand tour' or the 'grands récits' of the nineteenth century. Dorothy Richardson was one of the first writers of her generation to make such demands on her readers and to theorise the practice. Since then numerous writers have made a similar case for the interactive, participatory model of reading. Toni Morrison, talking about her own writing practice, is one recent example:

> to have the reader *feel* the narrator without *identifying* the narrator, or hearing him or her knock about, and to have the reader work *with* the author in the construction of the book – is what is important. What is left out is as important as what is there. To

describe sexual scenes in such a way that they are not clinical, not even explicit – so that the reader brings his (*sic*) own sexuality to the scene and thereby participates in it in a very personal way. (Morrison, 1983: 341)

Morrison's point is particularly useful for the sexual reticence of *Pilgrimage* - which I discuss later in Chapter 6 – and the question of exclusions and inclusions is also important. As I have argued above, Richardson leaves out certain kinds of information or clues normally found in the nineteenth-century novel. What she does not leave out is the details. The use of detail, I want to argue next, is one of the ways in which Richardson enables the reader 'to work *with* the author in the construction of the book'.

Reading the detail

To read *Pilgrimage* is to enter into a mass of detail, descriptive detail whose relevance to story, characterisation or theme is rarely made explicit. As critics frequently note, with irritation or pleasure, the book seems composed of minute observations of the particular, the details of colours, sounds, scents and textures as these are registered in Miriam's mind. It is often difficult to assign a meaning or function to any specific detail in relation to the structure, a mosaic of particularities makes it hard to see the overall pattern.

At one level Miriam's continual scrutiny of the details of objects, clothes, accents, furnishings, rooms, expresses her hermeneutic quest. She scans the particular world about her in an attempt to dissolve the old generalities, to find new meanings and new ways of reading. To read detail in this way is to find a thematic function for it. But there are many 'superfluous' details whose presence in the text is harder to justify in these terms.

At another level one might argue that the detail becomes a privileged point of contact between reader and text, a hook to which the reader may fasten their own fantasies, asssociations. At one point in the text the question of detail explicitly is raised as a problem for the heroine. Staying for the first time at the house of friends Alma and Hypo Wilson she sees, 'the copper candlestick, twisting beautifully up from its stout stem. What made it different from ordinary candlesticks? *What?* It was like a. . .gesture' (II, 112).

The detail of the candlestick 'twisting beautifully up from its stout stem' is never explained. It may suggest the stout body of Hypo Wilson and the way in which he is different from other men, it may represent simply her encounter with the Bohemian world, or it may signify neither of these. By activating the reader's own questions, the passage draws the reader into a parallel activity ('side by side') thus producing a collaborative reader. Reading the world and reading the text are paralleled so that in staging Miriam's attempt to read it, the passage itself operates as a 'gesture' to put the problems of signification (*what* signifies?) before the reader.

Roland Barthes, discussing the relation of detail and structure in nineteenth-century narratives, notes the existence of 'superfluous' detail:

> these details are scandalous (from the point of view of structure), or, even more disturbingly, they seem to be allied with a kind of narrative *luxury*, profligate to the extent of throwing up 'useless' details and increasing the cost of narrative information.[13]

According to Barthes, the inclusion of such descriptive detail in nineteenth-century narratives (trivial gestures, insignificant objects, superfluous dialogue) is used to produce a 'reality effect'; that is, excessive detail which is not integrated into the narrative or thematic codes serves to signify the category of 'the real'. Its function is to confirm the mimetic contract and to guarantee that the text is about the real world, and after a process of recognition and identification the reader can then interpret or give meaning to what has been identified.

But where there is an excessive proliferation of elements whose function seems purely referential, as in the six-page description of the room at the beginning of *The Tunnel*, the interpretive activity is problematised. The reader can construct the room (or object) but finds it difficult to construct a meaning for it: 'A mania of precision produces a thematique vide.'

Pilgrimage breaks with the nineteenth-century contract described by Barthes. It uses physical description, descriptive detail, repeatedly and at great length, not to ensure the 'reality effect' but to produce a resistance to meaning. Often

Richardson's use of detail is a device to delay or impede meaning-construction, to slow up the reading and 'hold up the development of the whole' (I, 11) which Richardson thought desirable in the novel. 'What one was assured were the essentials seemed to me secondary to something I could not then define, and the curtain dropping finalities entirely false to experience' (Richardson, 1959/1989: 139).

In terms of her aesthetic, the valorisation of the detail over the whole, the particular over the general may be necessary when the conventions governing the whole are 'false'. Or as Miriam claims in *Deadlock*:

> It was history, literature, the way of stating records, reports, stories, the whole method of statement of things from the beginning that was on a false foundation. (III, 218)

In other words, the particularism of *Pilgrimage* is a reaction to master narratives, to the conviction that all the major discursive modes – 'history, literature, the way of stating records' – were 'on a false foundation'. The point then is *not* to construct an alternative version of the master narrative, 'a feminine equivalent of the current masculine realism' (I, 9), but to lead the reader towards a new 'method of statement' for both literature *and* history.[14]

Reading the period

> 'You have in your hands material for a novel, a dental novel, a human novel and, as to background, a complete period, a period of unprecedented expansion in all sorts of directions... (...) in your outer world you've seen an almost ceaseless transformation, from the beginning of the safety bicycle to the arrival of the motor car and the aeroplane. With the coming of flying, that period is ended and another begins. You ought to document your period.' (Hypo to Miriam, IV, 397)

In the novel Miriam makes no reply to Hypo's advice and the method Richardson employs is very different from documentation. There *are* references to specific historical events in *Pilgrimage*: to the passing of the Education Act in *Backwater* which strikes terror into Miriam's untrained teacher's mind; to the trial of Oscar Wilde in *Honeycomb*; to the advent of horseless carriages, telephones and bicycles and the change

from gas to electricity; to suffragette marches and demon-
strations and imprisonment in Holloway, where Miriam visits
her friend Amabel and hears of 'someone fainting in a Black
Maria' (IV, 369); the Boer war, Ireland and the tensions between
England and Germany are also registered in the different
novel-chapters. Like Virginia Woolf, Richardson weaves her
allusions into the text as and when they impinge on the
consciousness of the heroine. Both women writers, one might
say, are concerned not simply with history as *events* but with
their subjects' lived relation to the historical, and both, like
Jane Austen before them, are accused of ignoring the decisive
historical events of their time.

Yet *Pilgrimage* may be read as a particularist history and, for
the collaborative reader concerned with social history, Miriam
Henderson is very much a girl of the period. Recent work by
feminist and social historians enables the reader to recognise
just how rich the novel is in details about women's education,
employment and living conditions for the single woman.[15]
Although it lacks the 'objective' narrative procedures demanded
by Lukacs, there is no 'negation of history' in *Pilgrimage*, the
history of the period is refracted through the mind of the
young woman, but that mind is itself constructed in historical
terms.

Richardson was not an exile or an *émigré* in the literal sense
that Pound, Eliot, Joyce and Conrad were, but because she
looks 'with the eyes of a stranger'[16] at the life of a middle-
class Englishwoman. It is her own life in the period 1891–1912,
read from another period, 1912–46. A past recreated as an
enormous present, the minutiae of daily life operate as a
'making strange', a defamiliarised image of the writer's own
class and the values and conditions it created for women
during a period of transition. The 'blow-up' of surface
appearances can be read then not as the naturalism deplored
by Lukacs, but as a way of looking for the 'deep forms and
shaping forces' which produce those appearances.

So, for example, *Pilgrimage* could be said to reflect upon
what Hobsbawm in *The Age of Empire* describes as 'the
uncertainties of the bourgeoisie'[17] through the consciousness
of a character forced out of her class (by the father's bankruptcy)
and into the job market – untrained, unskilled, without capital

or income. After a brief anachronistic 'impersonation' of the governess role, she becomes a clerical worker – part of the growing tertiary sector staffed mainly by the lower middle class and the upwardly mobile working class: an employee of the type of professional men she once met socially at tennis parties and musical evenings. The precision of detail about accent, voice and manner registers this class-displacement as both individual trauma and a presentation of the anxieties over demarcation lines within the bourgeoisie at the turn of the century. Poised below the 'secure' *rentier* class of her childhood, and above the 'abyss' of the working classes, Miriam Henderson looks at class divisions 'with the eyes of a stranger': with hatred and longing at the forms of class life she has left, with shame and anxiety at the shifts and deprivations of the lower middle-class world she has joined.

Existing in genteel poverty on her £1 a week, eating frugally in the new ABC restaurants serving the clerical world of London, her intellectual development is a conscious project to realise her condition and, the text suggests, less consciously a desire to redeem it. Unlike Forster's caricature of the bourgeois writer of the period, 'In came the dividends, up went the lofty thoughts', Dorothy Richardson locates her heroine's 'lofty thoughts' as both an attempt to understand and disguise the struggle for survival – when there are no dividends coming in. Miriam's reading is that of a dissenter, it casts light on the intellectual history of the period 1890–1912 and it enables Richardson to stage a dialogue with the dominant discourses of the day – on social, religious and political questions.

Take for example the issue of prostitution – an issue of general social concern in the period and of central importance for feminism. There are no social statistics or dramatic confrontations with prostitutes, but as Miriam circulates around the city, the issue is never far from her consciousness.[18] Her social identity as a single woman is worked out mainly in relation to the ideal of wife and mother but there is another model of femininity lurking in *Pilgrimage*. As Martha Vicinus says in *Independent Women*, the ideal wife and mother, the celibate single woman, and the promiscuous prostitute form a 'triangle of mythic possiblities' for women in the late Victorian and Edwardian periods.[19] Miriam's sense of men, like the feminism of the time, includes a fierce critique of male sexual behaviour. If in much nineteenth-century fiction by women there is an implicit identification with the prostitute, in the 1890s this becomes explicit. In the work of Sarah Grand and George Egerton, for example, attacks on 'male vice' begin to establish direct parallels between wives and prostitutes as victims of a male sexual rapacity – a rapacity which turns marriage into 'a legal prostitution, a nightly degradation, a hateful yoke'.[20]

The word 'prostitute' appears only twice in the text. In *The Tunnel*, the heroine, on one of her night wanderings, hears only the voice of 'an invisible woman' whose conversation suggests her profession, but 'The woman was there, there and real. . .there was no pretence about her' (II, 30). The woman's lack of pretence contrasts with that of her clients, but also perhaps with Miriam herself, whose problems with her sexuality and her position as a respectable single woman are considerable. Later in the same novel-chapter, two women friends living nearby reveal that their landlady is 'improper', visited by six or seven men in one evening, and that they are 'living in an improper house – the whole street's improper' (II, 84). After discussing the virtues of the 'absolutely self-respecting' landlady, the following dialogue takes place:

> 'I don't see that it's our business. Frankly I can't see that it has anything whatever to do with us. Do you?'
> [Miriam] 'Well, I don't know; I don't suppose it has really'. (II, 86)

Their conversation then continues, on men, marriage and the advantages of being single, working women: 'Freedom is life. We may be slaves all day and guttersnipes all the rest of the time but, ach Gott, we are free' (II, 92).

The limitations to Miriam's freedom, and her relation to prostitution are dramatised immediately afterwards, when Miriam is accosted on the walk back to her boarding house. She turns angrily on the man who disappears, leaving her to remember similar incidents. It is not the women, she decides, who are the problem, but the

> figures of men, dark, in dark clothes, presenting themselves, calling attention to themselves and the way they saw things, mean and suggestive, always just when things were at their loveliest. (II, 96)

There are further allusions to the issue in the next novel-chapter *Interim*, but it is not until *Deadlock*, when the man Miriam is in love with reveals his previous sexual experience, that the word prostitute is allowed to surface in her consciousness:

> The leer of a prostitute was. . .reserved. . .beautiful, (. . .) compared with the headlong desirous look of a man. The greed of men was something much more awful than the greed of a prostitute. (III, 208)

The connection between prostitutes and herself, which Miriam was unsure of in the earlier conversation, is now manifest in the person of the man she loves. Venereal disease is not mentioned, the narrative is taken up with her emotions of pain and disillusion, but Shatov's defence, 'Remember I did not know that you would come' (III, 207), several times repeated, makes a point about the double standard and its possible consequences for the middle-class wife or fiancée.

Later in *Pilgrimage*, when Miriam has broken off her relationship with Shatov, she returns to a coffee-shop visited with him and frequented by prostitutes. There she recalls,

> the moment of catching, as they sat down, the flicker of his mobile eyelid, the lively unveiled recognizing glance he had flung at the opposite table, describing its occupants before she saw them; the rush of angry sympathy; a longing to *blind* him; in some way to screen them from the intelligent unseeing glance of all the men in the world. (III, 279)

Her violent reaction signals that an identification between Miriam and 'them' is now established. The 'pure' and the 'fallen' woman are both constructed by the male gaze and it is this which Miriam wishes to 'blind'. When a few pages later in *Revolving Lights*, Miriam comes across an old woman begging in the gutter, 'Familiar. Forgotten. The last, hidden truth of London, spoiling the night' (III, 288), this time she does not cross the street nor fail to recognise the issue – of their common sexual predicament. The two women exchange a glance of 'naked recognition':

It was herself, set in her path and waiting through the years. Her beloved hated secret self, known to this old woman. (III, 289)

The method is oblique, the references scattered over hundreds of pages, but if one reads for it the issue is as 'there and real' in *Pilgrimage* as it is in the pages of Mayhew or Charles Booth.

Chapter Two

A form of quest

i found god in myself
& i loved her/ i loved her fiercely
(Ntozake Shange)

By their metaphors ye shall know them.
(Dorothy Richardson:
'The rampant metaphor')

In the summer of 1915, shortly before publication, the name
Pilgrimage was removed from the cover and title page of the
first volume when it was discovered that it was the title of
another novel. The first novel was thus issued as *Pointed Roofs*,
with an explanatory note stubbed in. From the first, Richardson
wanted her novel to be entitled *Pilgrimage*, with *Pointed Roofs*
as the subtitle, and as Part One of the whole (Fromm, 1977:
79). In this chapter I want to argue the importance of that title;
that the echo of Bunyan's *Pilgrim's Progress* signals a deliberate
and significant relationship between the two texts; that
Richardson's novel-sequence is in effect a revisionary allegory;
that far from being a shapeless 'stream of consciousness' novel,
based on simple chronology,[1] the form of *Pilgrimage* is framed
or patterned around a series of extended metaphors of life as
a journey – a journey with specific religious or spiritual
reference which only the word 'pilgrimage' could provide. This
title is the arch, spanning the thirteen individually titled novels
or 'chapters' and providing a framework for each of its parts.
How far the novel exceeds or escapes its frame can be grasped

only when the basic framing device is recognised.

As Christopher Hill says in a recent book on Bunyan, the metaphor of life as a journey is age-old while that of life as a pilgrimage goes back at least to the Middle Ages, if not further (Hill, 1988: 201, 379). The word 'pilgrimage' was not always simply a metaphor, of course, it once had a literal meaning as an institution of the Latin Church: in the medieval period it meant a journey to a sacred place undertaken as an act of religious devotion, either to venerate it, to ask for the fulfilment of a prayer, or as an act of penance. Between *The Canterbury Tales* (1387) and *Pilgrim's Progress* (1678), pilgrimages in fact became a thing of the past, not just in Protestant England where they were deemed a popish practice but in Catholic Europe too.[2] But what was written about the medieval pilgrimages survived as a source of imagery and fascination, for Romantic poets – Coleridge and Byron particularly – and the resonance of 'pilgrimage' as an image continued in various forms throughout the nineteenth century.

> By the 19th century, kinds of journeys which to the medieval mind would have had little to do with pilgrimage – the voyage of exploration, the chivalric quest, the sojourn, even the prodigal's return – had become conflated. The romantic quest, even when as with Byron it is called a pilgrimage, was a new and different image: it had become internalised. (Howard, 1980: 6)

In this new usage, the emphasis shifts from a physical to a mental landscape; the journey is marked by moral crises and choices, and the turning points and crossroads take place in a psychic terrain which looks back to the language of the Romantic poets and forward to that of Freud. It was, I think, these accumulated cultural meanings that Richardson wished to retain.

An allegorical journey

Pointed Roofs, the first volume of *Pilgrimage*, begins with a tracking shot of Miriam climbing the staircase to her room at the top of the house:

> Miriam left the gaslit hall and went slowly upstairs. The March twilight lay upon the landings, but the staircase was almost dark. The top landing was quite dark and silent. There was no one

about. It would be quiet in her room. She could sit by the fire and
be quiet and think things over until Eve and Harriett came back
with the parcels. She would have time to think about the journey
and decide what she was going to say to the Fräulein.

Her new Saratoga trunk stood solid and gleaming in the firelight.
To-morrow it would be taken away and she would be gone. . . .
The sense of all she was leaving stirred uncontrollably as she stood
looking down into the well-known garden. (I, 15)

Miriam is about to leave the family house in the south London
suburbs on a journey to the pointed roofs of Hanover, Germany,
where she will begin life as a teacher. But the reader is not
told this, nor who Eve, Harriett or the Fräulein are. After the
first sentence, the narrator who tells us of Miriam's physical
movements dissolves into the character who sees the darkness
of the staircase; her consciousness, the inner world of her
mental activity, is brought into focus before the narrator
reappears to provide a framing shot of Miriam looking down
at the garden from her bedroom window. As the chapter
continues, this process is repeated in a series of fluid
movements from 'outside' to 'inside' and back again. The
reader is not allowed to settle into a fixed viewing position
but is kept in a state of attention necessary in order to follow
the minute shifts in presentation.

The quiet naturalistic opening of *Pointed Roofs* rehearses a
method that Richardson was to use throughout the novel; it
also conceals what the overall title '*Pilgrimage*' reveals: its
possibilities as an allegorical fiction, a quest novel in which
the pilgrim sets out in search of a new sense of, and new
relation to, God. The Saratoga trunk and its various successors,
for example, accompany Miriam throughout her pilgrimage.
At the start of the sequence of novels, it is merely a concrete
sign of her impending departure, it confirms for the reader
the reference to 'the journey' that she intends to think about
when she reaches her room. The journey to Germany is the
first of many undertaken by the heroine and this scene of
setting forth is repeated many times; it is the preliminary to
journeys made on foot and by train, to the country and the
city, to fresh starts after false ones. The baggage that goes with
her changes its form but is always with her. It becomes, in
short, like the symbolic burden that the 'Graceless' pilgrim
must bear with her until she finds her salvation.[3]

Like Joyce's novel *A Portrait of the Artist as a Young Man*, published in the same year, the opening paragraphs operate as a sort of overture in which major themes and motifs are introduced. It figures the journey from the known to the unknown, the ascent from the communal areas ('gaslit hall') to solitary self-communing ('in her room'); the imagery of light and dark, of the baggage she must carry with her, of the 'well-known garden' which represents the enclosed spaces which call to her even as she leaves them, are repeated with variations in subsequent volumes. And the sound of music which triggers memories of the past – here the song *The Wearin' o' the Green* introducing the theme of exile and dispossession, is a constant feature of the text.

These motifs persist, in a dynamic and developed relation with other imagery, throughout *Pilgrimage* to the 'end' of the unfinished thirteenth novel, *March Moonlight*. The last pages find Miriam, having left the Quaker farm where she has solaced herself for a season,[4] installed in a new room, standing 'by the wide window of this sunlit top-back room' (IV, 655). The garden is invisible, she is 'alone with the sky' with only a 'lime tree and the tops of those poplars pointing up' in sight. Again at the top of a staircase, alone with light and shadows, listening to the sound of music – this time a Chopin ballade heard earlier in the delectable mountains of *Oberland* – the pilgrim begins a new stage of her journey: her life in writing. Although the imagery is modified to suggest a home-coming, the quest is still ongoing, the great journey to be continued. The pilgrimage here has no final destination within the text, it is not only as long as life itself, it *is* life itself, or 'the inside pattern of life' (III, 282) in so far as that can be represented in writing.

Richardson was not, of course, the only writer of her period to make extensive use of the journey metaphor. It is there in *The Voyage Out, To the Lighthouse, Ulysses, Passage to India,* 'Sailing to Byzantium', *The Heart of Darkness* and many other contemporary texts. Its literary popularity was no doubt reinforced by the fact that the late nineteenth century and early twentieth century was a period where travelling of all kinds increased, and where secular journeys of discovery by Schliemann, Scott and Shackleton were important elements within the national consciousness.[5] Darwin's earlier *Voyage of the Beagle* is an important reference point within *Pilgrimage* (I, 22 and II, 17), not only for the religious debates but also for the narrative method employed.[6] Whereas Joyce took his journey metaphors from the classical, pre-Christian poems of Homer and used these to structure his modern epic, Richardson's search for form took her to English religious writings of the seventeenth century – and specifically to those of the English Puritan, John Bunyan.

The early novels are studded with references to both the title and text of Bunyan's *Pilgrim's Progress*: thus at a moment of crisis in *Pointed Roofs* Miriam remembers a picture of Christian's battle with Apollyon the Destroyer from a childhood edition, and in despair decides that she 'belong[s] to Apollyon' (I, 170). At another point, in the second volume, she decides that '*Line upon Line* and *Pilgrim's Progress* were not meant for modern minds' (I, 262)[7] but returns a page later to the image of 'Christian's burden' (I, 263) and her own imperfections. In addition to the ubiquitous imagery of journeys and travelling – of ways, tracks, paths, routes, vistas, horizons, and gates, porches and enclosures – there are specific references to 'pilgrimage', to 'pilgrim baskets' and to Miriam's mysterious attraction to women who dress their hair in the 'flat-haired' Puritan fashion.[8] Such allusions may be read simply as a part of the story of the heroine's religious development: from the rejection of her parents' Church of England faith, through agnosticism and her encounters with Unitarian, Jewish and Quaker beliefs, to her search for 'inner light'. But they are, I think, more than this. Their cumulative effect is to take the reader back to the title and the nature of the parallels with the earlier text.

The traditional *Bildungsroman* usually starts with childhood, but Miriam's journey begins, like Christian's in *Pilgrim's Progress*, with her as an adult leaving her family. It is her spiritual not her psychological formation that we start from. Alienated from the family forms of belief ('The service I can't make head or tail of – think of the Athanasian', I, 20), she is in a state of spiritual despair as she sets out on 'her lonely pilgrimage' (I, 27). At the beginning of Bunyan's tale, his pilgrim also takes leave of his family and neighbours, fleeing

destruction and in search of 'Life! Life! eternal life!'. The
pointed roofs of Hanover signify, in a parallel reading, an
aspiration towards a higher form of existence as well as a
desire to escape the threatened destruction of her world. In
the next novel, significantly entitled *Backwater*, Richardson's
pilgrim returns from Hanover, as does Christian from Mount
Sinai, to the Slough of Despond, losing her religious hopes in
a mire of depression. In the next novel *Honeycomb*, whose title
is taken from Proverbs 5:3, she encounters the temptations of
luxury and the role-playing available in Vanity Fair. It is at
the end of this novel that Miriam's mother and companion,
herself a Christian in despair because 'God has deserted me'
(I, 489), kills herself with a kitchen knife. In *Pilgrim's Progress*
Christian loses his companion Faithful at Vanity Fair, after
Faithful has been scourged, buffeted and his flesh 'lanced with
knives' (p. 95).

The titles, imagery and incidents of Richardson's first three
novels signal the debt to Bunyan's narrative as explicitly as
does Joyce's 'Telemachia' to *The Odyssey*. As with Joyce, the
correspondences are often oblique and they can be traced
almost to the end of the sequence.

The Tunnel, for example, though its construction is modelled
on Dante's *Inferno*[9], also corresponds to Bunyan's Valley of the
Shadow of Death, whilst *Interim*, as its name implies, resembles
one of the resting-places in *Pilgrim's Progress* where the pilgrims
discuss their progress so far. The next three novels, *Deadlock*,
Revolving Lights and *The Trap* are all set in London which,
according to the heroine's state of mind, is imaged either as
a City of Destruction (I, 428) or the Celestial City (I, 416).
Bunyan for the most part also uses places as allegorical
equivalents to states of mind, except perhaps with Vanity Fair
which, in order to carry his critique of contemporary conditions,
goes beyond the purely allegorical. In the London setting,
Miriam's alternations between joy and despair, light and dark
passages, closely resemble those of Bunyan's hero and Bunyan
himself in his autobiography *Grace Abounding*. Her temptations
– the ease and security offered by conventional marriage –
parallel those offered to Christian by Mr Worldly Wiseman
and others. She is not tempted, though, to make her peace
with conventional religion: 'the Church will go on being a

Royal Academy of Males' (III, 323); the narrative instead stresses a growing sense of her own profanity – 'My everlasting profanity' (III, 507).

The Oxford English Dictionary defines 'profane' as:

> ad. L. profanus, lit. 'before (i.e. outside) the temple', hence 'not sacred', common, . . . characterised by disregard or contempt of sacred things; irreverent, blasphemous; impious, irreligious, wicked.

Not only is Miriam outside of Ruskin's temple, the family home, she finds her profanity separates her from most forms of organised religion. One of Miriam's spiritual problems, at the end of the eighth novel of *Pilgrimage*, is to redefine 'the sacred', to re-situate 'the temple', so that she will no longer be excluded or 'outside' it. The ninth volume, *Oberland*, gives her a glimpse, from the mountain tops, of how this might be done, and the next two entitled *Dawn's Left Hand* and *Clear Horizon* present her struggle to realise this new vision. No longer looking for the light above or beyond self, she begins to explore 'the strange new light within her' (IV, 153). In a series of mystical experiences, close to what Quakers called 'centring down',[10] the text stages the heroine's search for the divine presence *within* herself:

> at no matter what cost (. . .) she *would* reach that central peace; go farther and farther into the heart of her being and be there, as if alone, tranquilly, until fully possessed by that something within her that was more than herself. (IV, 219)

The journey imagery intensifies as Miriam discards the revolving lights of London with its sexual and literary false trails, abandons worldly companions and occupations, to prepare herself – horizons cleared – for entry into the New Life. Her travels in *Dimple Hill* take her away from her beloved London, to a Quaker community in Sussex, but they also take Richardson away from the narrative model offered by *Pilgrim's Progress*.

There are still textual links to Bunyan's 'Land of Beulah'; two references to a character called 'Beulah' (IV, 487, 492) and a scene in which Miriam learns to prune grapes which echoes the grape harvest in Bunyan's vineyards. In *Pilgrim's Progress*, when Christian and Hopeful enter the country of Beulah, they meet 'with abundance of what they had sought for in all their pilgrimage';[11] it is a land in which God rejoices over the pilgrims '*As the bridegroom rejoiceth over the bride*'.[12] It is from here that they see the gates of the 'Heavenly City' and a vision of eternal salvation. Although *Dimple Hill* is described in equivalent pastoral imagery, there is no bridegroom awaiting her here and no Shining Angels to herald her into the Celestial City. The family of Friends prevent her from marrying among them, she inadvertently blasphemes against their sacred beliefs (IV, 530–1) and they find her in the end too irreverent to become a Friend, and she is forced to leave. Despite their plain meeting-houses, she is once more outside 'the temple': 'the porch (. . .) was not open. . .she read there a challenge to her right of entry so clear as to seem spoken aloud' (IV, 650–1).

There is no equivalent to this development in *Pilgrim's Progress*. The doctrine of inner light and the religious individualism of Quaker belief, which appeal so powerfully to Miriam, cannot be fitted into the Puritan frame. Bunyan specifically denounces the Quaker doctrine of inner light in *Some Gospel Truths Opened* and elsewhere, as lacking the objective character of special revelation. His belief in Scripture as the foundation for Christian faith runs directly counter to the Friends' belief in personal experience rather than church or scripture, as the key to spiritual life.[13] At the end of *Pilgrim's Progress*, his pilgrims do indeed reach the destination promised in both the Old and New Testaments.

In *March Moonlight*, the last novel of *Pilgrimage*, Miriam unlike her biblical namesake, does not die in the desert of Zin but neither does she reach the Promised Land or Heavenly City. Despite the fact that the Friends' way is 'the best I've met' she decides that 'the thought of the missing letters [in their alphabet] makes the idea of a Quakerised world intolerable' (IV, 603). The repeated images of enclosure used of the Friends' community in *Dimple Hill*[14] link it back to the parental garden in *Pointed Roofs*, suggesting that it is just another garden, man-made and incomplete, from which she must once again set forth. The protagonist ceases to look for the inner light in Friends' meeting-houses, and begins to look elsewhere. Increasingly 'the strange journey down and down to the centre of being' (IV, 609) becomes associated with her attempts to write: 'Travel, while I write, down to that centre where everything is seen in perspective' (IV, 619). Thus, in a very Quakerly sense, Miriam takes her 'church' back on the road with her. The spiritual quest takes on a new direction as Miriam decides to record her life's pilgrimage in writing. Leaving the Puritan model behind her, Richardson launches her heroine into a typically modern world where writing itself is spiritualised. Writing becomes an act of devotion, of penance but also of contemplation:

> While I write, everything vanishes but what I contemplate. The whole of what is called 'the past' is with me seen anew, vividly. No, Schiller, the past does not stand 'being still'. It moves, growing with one's growth. Contemplation is adventure into discovery; reality. (IV, 657)

Until this point, the narrative parallels between *Pilgrimage* and *Pilgrim's Progress*, although not exact nor in strict sequence, are sustained and often detailed enough to operate as supporting structure, as scaffolding for the story of a modern woman's spiritual experience. Although in Miriam's view '*Pilgrim's Progress* [was] not meant for modern minds' (I, 262), Richardson clearly felt it had a reserve of power and sufficient cultural and religious resonance to provide a shape for her own construction. And this was, I think, her project – until the ending. Here she diverges and some of her difficulties with the writing of *March Moonlight*[15] may stem from her abandonment of *Pilgrim's Progress* as a narrative model. For complex reasons, Richardson could not provide Miriam with the kind of destination that Christian reaches. How then, could *Pilgrimage* end? For if life is simply a journey, its destination can only be death, but if life is imaged as a pilgrimage, a destination other than death must be in view. If neither death nor, for other reasons, marriage – the alternative fictional closure in the nineteenth-century novel – was appropriate, what ending could Richardson devise for her lifetime's work?

Journey narratives tend to divide into two main types: linear and circular.[16] In the linear model, the destination is a fixed and recognisable point which completes the journey, whereas in circular models, from *The Odyssey* onwards, where the destination is rejuvenative or restorative, the end of one cycle is the beginning of another. (Pilgrimages as an institution were in fact circular, since pilgrims tended to return home after going to Jerusalem or Canterbury, but pilgrimages as a literary metaphor tend to be linear in structure.[17]) In Bunyan's *Pilgrim's Progress* the journey 'from this world to the one that is to come' is linear, and the narrative is precisely divided into: 'The Manner of his Setting out; His Dangerous Journey; and Safe Arrival at the Desired Country'.

After the theological upheavals of the nineteenth century, described so graphically in *Pilgrimage*, the question of 'destination' became doubly problematic. The certainties about both salvation and afterlife, which inform Bunyan's allegory, were not as viable in a post-Darwinian age. Similarly, the image of a Heavenly City as the house of God which contains his 'real presence', would violate the symbolic logic of a novel which argues that God is *not* to be found in Heaven but is dispersed throughout Creation. Bunyan's contemporary, George Fox, the Founder of the Society of Friends, whose religious teachings are crucial to Miriam's conception of her relation to God, could not offer any alternatives in the way of narrative structure. His *Journal*, which Richardson used for her biography of Fox, is organised like other spiritual autobiographies of the seventeenth century, into Pre-Conversion, Conversion, Calling and Ministry.

Richardson's last unfinished volume takes the heroine towards a destination which is a form of renewal. The title *March Moonlight* echoes the March twilight with which *Pointed Roofs* began: the heroine is positioned in another suburban London room, using the same imagery of light/shadow, sky and garden, as outlined earlier. Season, setting and motifs all work to suggest that this is not so much a 'Safe Arrival' but another 'Setting out', this time with the pilgrim as writer. The vocational aspect of writing is registered with Miriam's recognition that 'To write is to forsake life' (IV, 609) recalling the biblical promise that: 'He that findeth his life shall lose it: and he that loseth his life for my sake shall find it'.[18] As in Goethe's *Wilhelm Meister*, there are definite acknowledgements in this last volume, that the text which Miriam begins to write at the end of *Pilgrimage*, is the novel we are reading. This brings not only Miriam but the reader to full circle; the journey ends where it began. 'In my end is my beginning.'

A woman's quest

From beginning to end, the spiritual theme in *Pilgrimage* is intricately bound up with questions of gender. Miriam's mind fastens on sexual difference 'like a horse-leech at the Vein', as Bunyan said of his own mind and the divine. Her feminism informs her critique of religious institutions, but equally, her focus on women's experience in a male-dominated world has a clearly articulated spiritual dimension. The critique of gender relations is powered 'by an essentially spiritual vision of what life should be about', says Dennis Brown in *The Death of God*.

In the early volumes, the rejection of organised religion is both feminist and anti-formalist ('Why could people not get at God direct?' I, 457). Miriam may cease to read her Bible, but she does not reject the idea of God as such, only the male idea of God. Her 18-year-old mind is bewildered and dismayed at the idea of a universe without God:

> There were people. . . distinguished minds, who thought Darwin was true.
>   No God. No Creation. The struggle for existence. Fighting . . .Fighting. . .Fighting. Everybody groping and fighting. . .Fraulein. Some said it was true. . .some not. They could not both be right. It was probably true. . .Only old-fashioned people thought it was not. Just that – monkeys fighting. But who began it? Who made Fraulein? Tough leathery monkey. . .
>   Then nothing matters. Just one little short life. (I, 169–70)

The discovery of Darwin and evolutionary theory are traumatic for her, and the middle volumes of *Pilgrimage* present her obsession with the conflicts which dominated the late Victorian period: science *or* religion, materialism *or* idealism. Huxley and Spencer's application of evolutionary theories to the social sphere outrage her sense of herself as a woman and an individual; she is unwilling to see individual life as 'one little short life' and collective life simply as a great evolutionary power struggle – 'Fighting'. If 'religion in the world had nothing but insults for women' (II, 222), science seemingly reduces them to 'half-human creatures' (II, 220). Although at one point, Miriam reflects on her father's acquaintance with Faraday who successfully combined Christian faith with his work as a scientist, 'science' is consistently equated with a kind of masculine scientistic discourse which excludes 'religion'. Trapped within the great binary opposition of the period ('Either science or religion. They can't both be true' II, 237), Miriam eventually decides that both are untrue because incomplete, that both leave out something essential. They share, she argues, the characteristic of male discourse: a narrow rationalism which reduces life to a series of linear propositions from which surrounding circumstances and connections are left out and 'life itself' is missing:

> Someone will discover some day that Darwin's conclusions were wrong, that he left out some little near obvious thing with big results, and his theory, which has worried thousands of people nearly to death, will turn out to be one of those everlasting mannish explanations of everything which explain nothing. (III, 110)

Musing on the mentality which seems to govern all her male friends, the lawyers, medical men, even writers like Hypo Wilson, she comes to recognise that her problem is not just with men but with the culture, writing itself: 'It was history, literature, the way of stating records, reports, stories, the whole method of statement of things from the beginning that was on a false foundation' (III, 218). The result of this 'false foundation' *Pilgrimage* implies, is a discursive system in which neither 'God' nor 'women' can be adequately represented. Miriam's position as a woman, her gender, may be what alerts her to these gaps, but in the text the discovery is given a standing independent of her motives. Her rage and confusion are clearly and fully exhibited in dialogue and the interior monologue sections of the novel, but her misery and dejection at what science and religion offer women provide the grounds for the growth of a developing mind.

In the next stage of the search her attempts to articulate the missing element are repeatedly troubled by another duality *within* herself. 'Men', whether in the pulpit or laboratory, may be responsible for the omissions, for the very death of God, but as the heroine says, more than once, 'I am as much a man as a woman' (III, 221). The daughter of a Christian mother and Darwinian father, she inherits the dual legacies of their belief and unbelief, together with the 'criss-cross heredity' (III, 220) of biology and temperament (see III, 247–51); further, as a woman with a strong identification with her father, reluctant to define herself simply as 'woman', she is simultaneously fascinated by the intellectual systems she finds so repugnant. Culturally, biologically and emotionally, she is forced to recognise how she is implicated in the man-made world and the man-made religion of her Puritan ancestors:

> Within me...the *third* child, the longed-for son, the two natures, equally matched, mingle and fight? It is their struggle that keeps me adrift, so variously attracted, now here, now there? Which will win?... Feeling so identified with both, she could not imagine either of them set aside. Then her life *would* be the battlefield of her two natures. (III, 250).

In the early novels, while Miriam is hostile to 'women', her intimations that 'Women were of God in some way' (I, 404), operate as a block to her spiritual development. She sees the link between 'the hateful world of women' (I, 22) and what she later calls 'the God of the patriarchate' (III, 328) as a symbiotic relationship which upholds existing power relations between men and women: 'Women. They smiled at God. But they all flattered men' (II, 267). This has two effects on her thinking: on the one hand, it confirms her paranoid fantasy of these two 'creators', God and women, as 'bad parents' in league against her; and on the other hand, it enables her to see the love of God for His/Her creatures in terms of the parents whom at this stage she wishes to be independent of, whom she left home to get away from:

> The love of God was like the love of a mother; always forgiving you, ready to die for you, always waiting for you to be good. It was mean. (I, 391)

It is only as she works through the negative projections onto 'women', and the feminine within herself, that she can begin to make a positive link between God's Being and her own existence or being, between God's love and her own ability to love. This, though, involves a radical reorientation of the heroine's ideas about both God and the feminine, and the last three volumes of *Pilgrimage* focus on this process of reorientation, this stage of her pilgrimage, in all its psychological and spiritual complexity.

The initial point in this process is presented at some length in *Clear Horizon* (IV, 295–308). Miriam is at a concert with

Michael Shatov, the friend and lover whom she has decided
not to marry (and has in fact decided should marry her closest
friend Amabel). It is after this double renunciation of human
love, in a mood of extreme 'bleakness' (IV, 297) that a musical
phrase triggers,

> the certainty that elsewhere, far away in some remote region of
> consciousness, her authentic being was plunged in a timeless
> reality within which, if only she could discover the way, she might
> yet rejoin it. . . . (IV, 298)

The imagery of the journey intensifies as Miriam's efforts to
push beyond the barriers of her everyday consciousness are
described. Her mystical experience is an attempt to authorise
a new self which, paradoxically, pre-exists her present one,
and is indeed 'her authentic being'. Again, it is the old
'profane' self which is about to become re-born, re-authorised
as the 'sacred' reality for which she has been searching
throughout her pilgrimage. The possible meaning of this
mystical experience, for Miriam and for the reader, depends
on the whole section (and ultimately of course on the whole
novel), but something of its complexity can be seen in the
following paragraphs:

> But from within the human atmosphere all about her came the
> suggestion that this retreat into the centre of her eternal profanity,
> if indeed she should ever reach it again, was an evasion whose
> price she would live to regret. Again and again it had filled her
> memory with wreckage. She admitted the wreckage, but insisted
> at the same time upon the ultimate departure of regret, the way
> sooner or later it merged into the joy of a secret companionship
> restored; a companionship that again and again, setting aside the
> evidence of common sense, and then the evidence of feeling, had
> turned her away from entanglements by threatening to depart, and
> had always brought, after the wrenching and the wreckage,
> moments of joy that made the intermittent miseries, so rational
> and so passionate and so brief, a small price to pay.
> With a sense of battle waged, though still all about her, much
> nearer than the protesting people, was the chill darkness that yet
> might prove to be the reality for which she was bound, she drew
> back and back and caught a glimpse, through an opening inward
> eye, of a gap in a low hedge, between two dewy lawns, through
> which she could see the features of some forgotten scene, the last
> of a fading twilight upon the gloomy leaves of dark, clustered
> bushes and, further off, its friendly glimmer upon massive tree-
> trunks, and wondered, as the scene vanished, why the realization

of a garden as a gatherer of growing darkness should be so deeply
satisfying, and why these shadowy shrubs and trees should move
her to imagine them as they would be in morning light. (IV, 299)

In a spiritual sense, this is a scene of rebirth. The first
paragraph considers the high costs of journeying beyond the
empirical world of 'common sense' and 'feeling', and the
second paragraph, with the movement through darkness
towards the light and the birth-canal imaged as 'a gap in a
low hedge, between two dewy lawns', works to suggest that
Miriam is leaving the uterine 'sea of humanity' (IV, 297) where
she has been developing to enter the world as a new 'being'.
As Shirley Rose comments in her reading of it: 'The birth-
thrust is into the self' and the 'opening inward eye' signals
the arrival of a new vision.[19] But the passage is so constructed
that it lies open to other readings, in which for example the
first paragraph is not merely the preamble to the spiritual
experience of the second, but provides a possible explanation
of it as indeed a 'retreat' and 'evasion'. Mystical experience
for this woman, as for others, offers a transcendence of a
constricted social world. The presentation of Miriam's religious
and psychological states licenses both kinds of reading. The
ambiguity is built into the presentation of Miriam's visionary
experiences, but emerges particularly strongly in the notion of
'being' as used by Richardson.

In *Clear Horizon*, *Dimple Hill* and *March Moonlight*, the
oppositions set up in the earlier novels between religion and
science are reworked in terms of the dialectic between 'Being
and Becoming'. The Darwinian emphasis on the evolutionary
character of existence – at the expense of what is unchanging
– is linked by Miriam with 'becoming' as a male or masculine
quality, whereas 'being', the eternal continuous aspect, is
increasingly linked with women and the feminine outlook.
The traditional metaphysical opposition is gendered, one might
say, in a traditional way. Thus Hypo Wilson, the rationalist
with a belief in scientific socialism (H.G. Wells, the model for
Wilson, was a student of Huxley) becomes the spokesman for
'becoming' and antagonist to Miriam's search for 'being' in
the universe. Richardson uses their relationship, often to
great comic effect, to dramatise being and becoming as two
diametrically opposed visions of life: if 'his world of ceaseless

"becoming"' (IV, 361) is anathema to her, her concern with 'the mere existence of anything, anywhere' (IV, 362) is for him mere 'turnip emotion' (IV, 172). Their arguments drive them apart, but enable her to realise her position:

> Being versus becoming. Becoming versus being. Look after the being and the becoming will look after itself. Look after the becoming and the being will look after itself? Not so certain. Therefore it is certain that becoming depends upon being. Man carries his bourne within himself, and is there already, or he would not even know that he exists. (IV, 362)

The logic of this position takes Miriam further away from 'common sense', from 'feeling', from thinking even, into the kind of spiritual exercise which she compares to a 'mining operation' (IV, 498).

In *Dimple Hill* she undertakes these operations among Friends, convinced that 'where two or three are gathered together in my name, there am I - *in the midst of them*' (IV, 498). Miriam gives the prayer of St Chrysostom, quoted here and earlier, a special significance. She seeks a core of being, an 'I', amidst the myriad selves of her past 'becomings'; only in the contemplation of these past states, she feels, will she find the principle of unity running through her life. Since she calls this point a 'recognition', it implies the finding of something pre-existent, not a construction, and not an origin as such. In Quaker terms this core of being might be called the 'seed of God', which in so far as it is of God, would pre-exist Creation and thus have no point of origin. This would in turn link it back to the religious meaning of the Chrysostom prayer, for the core of being she hopes to reach will be the spirit of God in wo/man and thus a part of God's Being.[20]

The representation of Miriam's later spiritual development in the text presents special problems, over and above the usual difficulties of writing of mystical experience (some of which I return to in the discussion of subjectivity in Chapter 6). If, as is argued earlier, the dominant scientistic discourse has marginalised the questions she considers central, then the object of Miriam's quest is the inexpressible, the spirit of 'life itself': 'He seems to say spirit when he means life. Breath is more than words; the fact of breathing. . .' (III, 173).

It is a part of Richardson's project, one might say, to

emphasise these representational problems. Indeed, in a sense, as I argue more fully later, the whole stylistic project of *Pilgrimage* is to assert a counter-discourse expressive of the kind of spiritual holism her heroine seeks. To represent this dilemma, Richardson supplements her Biblical sources with philosophical and religious traditions which are themselves on the margins: Emerson, Fox and the writings of the seventeenth-century German visionary, Jacob Boehme referred to in *The Tunnel* (II, 283). But for the most part, the presentation of this stage of Miriam's pilgrimage concentrates on her spiritual technique, on the pathway rather than the destination:

> Be still and *know*. Still in mind as well as in body. Not meditating, for meditation implies thought. Tranquil, intense concentration that reveals first its own difficulty, the many obstacles, and one's own weakness, and leads presently to contemplation, recognition.
>   Bidding her mind be still, she felt herself once more at work, in company, upon an all-important enterprise. This time her breathing was steady and regular and the labour of journeying, down through the layers of her surface being, a familiar process. Down and down through a series of circles each wider than the last, each opening with the indrawing of a breath whose outward flow pressed her downwards towards the next, nearer to the living centre. Again thought touched her, comparing this research to a kind of mining operation. For indeed it was not flight. There was resistance from within, at once concrete and buoyant, a help and a hindrance, alternately drawing her forward and threatening, if for an instant her will relaxed, to drive her back amongst the distractions of the small cross-section of the visible world by which she was surrounded. (IV, 498–9)

In this example, the passage starts with a quote from the 46th Psalm ('Be still then, and know that I am God'), then moves on to describe the contemplative method in a circle-image borrowed from Emerson; it also seems to draw on William James's definition of mysticism as combining the ineffable, the noetic, transience and passivity.[21] This spiritual exercise is conducted at a Quaker meeting, and described in some detail as part of the 'distractions' to which she succumbs. The attempt to approach 'Reality' is unsuccessful here.

In the last unfinished novel, *March Moonlight*, a new 'clue to the nature of reality' (IV, 612) appears in the form of a woman. This figure, a woman called Jean whom Miriam meets in the Swiss mountains, links back to all the women she has loved in her previous lives: her mother, her sister Harriett, Eleanor Dear and Amabel. Unlike the other characters there is apparently no known prototype for this figure in Richardson's own life; she seems to be an imaginary composite (possibly named for 'John' of the Gospels):

> Jean. Jean. Jean. My clue to the nature of reality. To know that you exist is enough. (IV, 612)

She is a 'clue' in the sense that she teaches her disciple Miriam the possibilities of love without either desire or possession, without 'clutching' (IV, 575) and that realisation enables her to enter into a new contemplative phase. Miriam's love for this figure is at first all too human but she learns, painfully, and typically alone, a different kind of love. In psychoanalytic terms this might be called a fantasy of unconditional love, in religious terms 'Jean' reads as the embodiment of human love which most nearly approaches God's love for human beings: 'perfect love'.

By struggling to see herself as Jean 'the permanent forgiver' (IV, 607) sees her and loves her, Miriam begins what for her are the most difficult tasks: loving herself and loving others as herself, with full forgiveness: 'From hell, heaven is inaccessible until one has forgiven oneself' (IV, 607). Only then, and only at certain moments, can she realise the reality of herself and others:

> And for the first time I realized that my porch was Harriett's also(. . .) There she was, gazing, in solitude, into her own life, realizing it as it slipped, with the approach of marriage, away into the past, realizing that soon it would be inaccessible.
> Within the depths of that moment I seemed to gaze into her being. Aware of it as if it were my own. For the first time I realized the unique, solitary person behind the series of appearances that so far had represented in my mind the sister called Harriett. And as the scene vanished, its curious darkling light spread, fading, across the world, showing me, as it moved, dim unknown figures as real as she. (IV, 608–9)

Paradoxically, in a novel renowned for the egocentricity of its heroine, one of the goals of that heroine turns out to be the transcendence of egoism, an aspiration to realise the other not just as oneself, but as 'God' might see them. Such a project seems impossible because it places before human beings a paradigm of ultimate objectivity, of love as the acceptance of things and people as they are.[22] It is a notion of the Spirit, which rather than being projected onto God 'out there', is acknowledged as a central part of human aspirations. In other words, Miriam comes to realise that the only God she will find in church, is the one she brought in with her, that she is only profane and outside the temple in so far as she is alienated from the Spirit within.

Miriam's critique of religious institutions and her recognition of the Bible as a 'culture' not truth links *Pilgrimage* with the work of contemporaries in Britain and America – contemporaries like Elizabeth Cady Stanton whose *Women's Bible* first appeared in 1895. Her conception of the Spirit and the contemplative experience as a journey towards love, on the other hand, links her with a long line of feminine mystics who would also maintain:

> It is a knowledge of the vital principle of relatedness – love – that binds all things, the principle that is the internal dynamic of the Godhead itself.[23]

As one can see from passages like the one cited above, the mystical path followed by the heroine and outlined in *Pilgrimage* exceeds, in every sense, the framework of Bunyan's Puritan theology. It also in many respects exceeds the grasp the present reader, or perhaps any reader unversed in the new theology. However this, I would argue, is part of the design of *Pilgrimage*: to draw the reader into a textual pilgrimage of his or her own which would take them beyond their usual frame of reference, beyond the 'hard visible horizon' of what Blake calls their 'single vision'.

Chapter Three

London: space for a woman

I find it necessary to keep two books. . .otherwise the autobiography is eaten up by statistics of wages, hours of work. . . – no room for the general history of a woman's life.

(Webb, 1982: 220)

when evoking the name and destiny of women, one thinks more of the *space* generating and forming the human species than of *time*, becoming or history.

(Kristeva, 1986: 190)

Pilgrimage gives a lot of textual space to women: in the most obvious sense, more than 2,000 pages are devoted to what Beatrice Webb feared would get squeezed out of her diaries – the 'history of a woman's life'. It also offers an examination of the public and private 'space' available to a woman in late Victorian and Edwardian England, and it stages a woman's search for an identity and meaning for her life in spatial imagery which, while it often has a concrete literal reference, carries psychic and social implications beyond the literal. Freud, in 'Civilisation and its discontents' (1961: 69–70), used the city of Rome as an image for the mind of man; Richardson, I shall argue, uses the city of London to represent the mind and the body of a woman.

For Miriam Henderson is a traveller who, in the narrative, lives for the most part in one place: London. Seven of the thirteen novels are set in one small area of London, the streets and squares between the British Museum and the Euston Road, flanked on the east by Judd Street and on the west by the Tottenham Court Road. Where Bunyan moves his pilgrims at will – from the flat fields of Bedfordshire to the hills of the Old Testament Palestine – according to the needs of the allegory, Richardson's use of her London setting is geographically as detailed as Joyce's use of Dublin in *Ulysses*. The novel is often unspecific about time and dates, but places are described with great precision. The descriptions register, for example, the changing fortunes of many eighteenth-century London houses, from town houses for the gentry to boarding-houses for the clerks, tourists and emigrés in the late Victorian period. The sense of the historical, of the epoch, is *materialised* into spatial terms, so that the streets and houses of London become 'materialized history' as Bakhtin said of Balzac's depictions of houses (Bakhtin, 1981: 247). She is the first woman novelist in the history of the English novel to give the city this kind of attention and as John Cowper Powys says, 'Dorothy Richardson is a Wordsworth of the city of London' (Powys, 1931: 19–20).

In Bunyan's story, each new moment of time, or stage of the pilgrimage, is represented by a new place; for example the onset of a spiritual crisis is signified by his arrival at Doubting Castle. In *Pilgrimage*, although certain temporal stages are marked by a change of place (Miriam's visit to Oberland, for example), the passing of time and the stages of her pilgrimage are usually represented by variations in the spatial imagery used to describe the same place: London. All pilgrimages of course have a spatial and temporal dimension, since journeys take place in time and space, but the spatial element is given a special importance in the organisation of Richardson's novel. She creates a new kind of temporality, what Kristeva calls 'Women's Time', in which space and the things in it displace the usual registration of linear time.[1]

Bakhtin, in 'Forms of time and the chronotope in the novel', calls the combination of temporal and spatial elements in the novel a 'chronotope' (literally a 'time-space'). He argues that chronotopes, for example chronotopes of the road or the encounter, function 'as the primary means for materializing time in space. . .a centre for concretizing representation, a force giving body to the entire novel'.[2] In the chronotope of the road (or journey),

> the spatial and temporal paths of the most varied people – representatives of all social classes, estates, religions, nationalities, ages – intersect at one spatial and temporal point. People who are normally kept separate by social and spatial distance can accidentally meet;. . .human fates and lives combine with one another in distinctive ways, even as they become more complex and more concrete by the collapse of *social distances*. (Bakhtin, 1981: 243)

London, in *Pilgrimage*, serves as just such a meeting point. Removed from the sheltered, socially homogeneous suburbs of her middle-class family, Miriam here encounters representatives from various classes, religions, nationalities: Russians and Canadians, Jews and atheists, Fabians and feminists, the working-class Sissie and the aristocratic Amabel. London is her university in which she learns about the social heterogeneity that lies outside the enclosed world of her suburban girlhood. Within the text it is also a means of representing late Victorian and Edwardian England in the Age of Empire. In an age of consumption as never before, Miriam is shown taking friends to see the Elgin Marbles in the British Museum, listening to her employers discussing diamonds from South Africa before the Boer War, passing the shop-windows of Regent Street, looking in at the products culled from all corners of the British Empire. Her gaze registers these items like the fixed eye of a camera:

> Shops passed by, bright endless caverns screened with glass. . .the bright teeth of a grand piano running along the edge of a darkness, a cataract of light pouring down its raised lid; forests of hats; dresses, shining against darkness, bright headless crumpling stalks; sly, silky ominous furs; metals cold and clanging, brandishing the light; close prickling fire of jewels. . .strange people who bought these things, touched and bought them. (I, 417)

The libraries, museums, shops and people of London, encountered on her walks around London, all testify to the rich diversity of the imperial city. Again, Bakhtin's comments are relevant: 'the road is always one which passes through *familiar territory*, and not through some exotic alien world. . .it is the *social heterogeneity* of one's own country that is revealed and depicted' (1981: 245). Alienated from the familial hearth and from a position as consumer, Miriam looks with 'the eyes of a stranger' at familiar territory, the physical and social space in which she moves and has her being. It is largely this treatment of London as 'social space', dense with details of English social life in the 1890s and the years before the First World War, which for the collaborative reader conveys the period. In this respect, *Pilgrimage* does follow Hypo's advice to 'document your period' (IV, 397) but it does it in a radically different way from that used by H.G. Wells in, say, *Ann Veronica*.

Richardson's presentation differs from that of Hypo Wilson, but also from other, autobiographical, writings by women in this period. It differs notably, for example, from the ways in which suffragette autobiographies document their period and a comparison with these sheds particular light on the question of public and private space. The struggle towards the enfranchisement of women, as feminist historians have noted,[3] produced large numbers of autobiographies, memoirs and life stories of various kinds by the Pankhursts, Annie Kenney, Emmeline Pethick-Lawrence, Hannah Mitchell and many others; apart from its other effects, the suffrage struggle drew many women into writing. Like *Pilgrimage*, most of these accounts were written later, in the 1920s and 1930s, and like *Pilgrimage* many of them have a quest motif and feature the problem of women's search for identity in a changing world[4]. *Pilgrimage* also treats the suffrage question, in Miriam's visit to Amabel in Holloway after a street demonstration (IV, 357–9 and 369–70), but as a minor episode in a much longer narrative. It gives much less space to what is a major concern to the suffragette writers, and constructs that space in a very different way.

In suffragette autobiographies, the public and historical events are given primacy. Since these are specifically concerned with women's struggle to redefine themselves as *political* subjects, the *personal* elements are given minimal representation. Recounting the struggle to enter and gain recognition within the public world, to gain entry to that most 'public' of spaces, the Houses of Parliament, the autobiographies repress areas of private conflict, doubt and difficulty – except in so far as these illustrate the case for suffrage. For example, when

Emmeline Pankhurst tells the story of overhearing her father's wish that she had been born a boy, the point is made but immediately closed off by a statement that she, Emmeline, had never felt such a wish (no penis envy here!). Or, as in the brisk paragraph describing her 'nearly ideal' relations with her husband, the personal detail is included, it seems, only to confound the stereotype of suffragists as emotionally disappointed women.[5] Similarly, the hysterical reaction experienced by Emmeline Pethick-Lawrence on being enclosed in a 'Black Maria', and her sufferings in prison, are swiftly passed over: at the narrative level there is little or no space allotted to these subjective experiences.[6] Their autobiographies, one might say, were in service to the political (not the personal), to their convictions (not their uncertainties) and the personal and the political are kept in separate compartments.

Although there are exceptions to this pattern, like Hannah Mitchell's *The Hard Way Up*, these feminist autobiographies in general observe the conventional boundaries between public and private realms, suggesting continuity with nineteenth-century feminism and its analysis of women's oppression in terms of public rights. In Richardson's novel-sequence, however, the boundary-lines between public and private domains are continually disturbed, transgressed, and exposed as part of the man-made conventions entrapping the heroine and the reader. *Pilgrimage* in this way anticipates the claim of later feminists that 'the personal is political'. What is left out, repressed, or evident only as tensions and contradictions in the suffragists' autobiographies is brought into focus via Miriam's consciousness. So, for example, *her* father's wish that she had been a boy, and the consequences of his desire on the inner life of the heroine, are traced through the entire sequence. The fictionalising of her autobiographical subject (the use of the third person and other devices) gave Richardson, perhaps, the liberty to treat what is missing from many of her fellow feminists' writing and to present the 'personal' material in a new and dialectical relationship with the social conditions that Hypo urges Miriam to document. Thus the kind of splitting between public and private, inner and outer worlds, described by Beatrice Webb, is consistently challenged.

Women's sphere

The concept of separate spheres for men and women was central to nineteenth-century gender ideology and to the creation of the middle-class home during the period;[7] women's sphere was the home, a 'sacred place' removed from the thoroughfares and market places of the Victorian business world. In Ruskin's now classic formulation,

> home. . .is the place of peace; the shelter, not only from all injury, but from all terror, doubt, and division. . .a sacred place, a vestal temple, a temple of the hearth watched over by household gods. (Ruskin, 1865: 59)

The sacredness of the home does not lie in its bricks and mortar, but in the presence of the woman within it – the 'true' woman:

> Wherever a true wife comes, this home is always round her. The stars only may be over her head, the glow-worm in the night-cold grass may be the only fire at her foot, but home is yet wherever she is; and for a noble woman, it stretches far around her. . . . (*ibid.*)

This ideology of woman – home – woman, which dominates the representation of women in the nineteenth-century novel, also provides the terms in which women's later aspirations could be textualised. As Martha Vicinus and others have pointed out,[8] the spatial imagery of rooms and houses are extensively employed in late nineteenth- and early twentieth-century writing by women; rooms and houses remain central figures to signify the social and psychic space occupied by women. The house is no longer imaged as a simple refuge or shelter from the world, it is often now a prison or cage. It is no longer a question of sheltering from the world's doubts and divisions, but of whether the house, the woman's sphere, can be re-organised to provide women with a room of her own, or at least a room with a view, or whether indeed she must move out – as does Nora in *A Doll's House*. The slamming of the door at the end of that play suggests that for Nora to be reborn she must move out of the space traditionally demarcated as the woman's sphere. Her exit signals the end of an era, but it also inaugurates a new set of images of the home or house – topographical possibilities which Richardson, an admirer of Ibsen, put to use in her writing.

Pilgrimage begins where *A Doll's House* ends, with the heroine's departure from the family home. She like Nora has stepped outside of Ruskin's 'sacred place'. It is not, however, until four years later (in *The Tunnel*) that she finds a room of her own. Until this point in the narrative she either shares a room with other teachers, as in *Pointed Roofs* and *Backwater*, or, as a governess, occupies the spare room at the house of the Corries in *Honeycomb*. The acquisition of a room of her own in a London boarding-house, separate from her place of work, has several levels of significance. In class terms it registers Miriam's new economic position as a wage earner, previously masked by her 'live-in' situations. It thus marks her downward mobility from being 'the daughter of a gentleman' to becoming one of the employed. 'One of the greatest hardships of the comparatively poor members of the middle class', say Davidoff and Hall, 'was to go into lodgings in other people's houses.'[9] In gender terms, it marks a break from the Ruskinian ideal of the woman and a step towards independence and self-development. For in the Victorian model, a young woman remained in her father's home until she married and moved into her husband's home, as indeed Miriam's two sisters Sarah and Harriett do. At the spiritual and psychological levels, the new room, 'half dark shadow and half brilliant light' (II, 13), in which Miriam ritually opens the windows and washes her hands while listening to the bells of St Pancras church, becomes itself a metonymic image for the self, the 'beloved hated secret self' (III, 289) that it is a part of her quest to discover. Miriam's comment, 'I left home to get here' (II, 13) directs the reader towards the figurative significance of the room, for her and for her story.

The first chapter of *The Tunnel* describes in great detail Miriam's first impressions of the room and its contents. Each item of furniture is registered – down to the number of drawers in the room, the alternation of light and shadow, the smell of the dusty counterpane, the hiss of the gas light, the feel of the wallpaper and so on. The synaesthetic evocation of a small room in these passages is characteristic of Richardson's descriptive method and the problems this poses for the reader. In a traditional reading, the physical description of the room here serves to create an effect of realism about the setting, it further characterises the heroine, and it carries thematic points already established and some yet to be introduced. The 'black bars of the little grate' in the empty fireplace (II, 14), for example, are later in the text picked up as a contrast to the well-built fires of her childhood in her father's home where bottles of green chartreuse stood warming in front of the hearth (IV, 250). The 'hearth', in *Pilgrimage*, is not allowed to stand as a symbol of national and familial unity, but is used to represent different states, physical as well as mental, in the heroine's existence. The unified 'hearth' of Victorian iconography is broken down into a series of particular 'grates' and fireplaces, tended by servants in middle-class houses, giving off more or less heat, and bearing a rather different set of meanings. Nevertheless, the detail and length of the description may still appear, to many readers, in excess of the needs of characterisation, theme or setting. Virginia Woolf claims, in her review of *The Tunnel*, that these details 'never reach that degree of significance which we, perhaps unreasonably, expect'.[10] Richardson's mode of writing raises complex questions about 'significance' and the reader's 'expectations' discussed above (Chapter 1) and the relation of detail to space has a special significance.

In the chapter of *The Tunnel* just mentioned, the room is not the only space given detailed presentation; within the boarding-house, the staircase and each of its landings (there are three), the exact degree of light and shade, the colour of the wallpaper and floor-covering are all identified with great particularity. Further, the outer spaces surrounding the house, what Miriam can see and hear of London from the window of her room, are also given several paragraphs. Nothing that the heroine perceives, it seems, is to be *unbestimmt*. As Katherine Mansfield complained: 'everything being of equal importance to her, it is impossible that everything should not be of equal unimportance.'[11] To the economic short-story writer, as to Woolf, the amount of detail seemed merely excessive. I would argue, however, that here as elsewhere, Richardson's use of detail is not an unfortunate lapse into prolixity but a strategy which has quite specific effects on the way one reads the novel.

First, as the Foreword to the 1938 edition makes clear,[12] it is a *deliberate* strategy designed to delay and impede the interpretive activity, so that the reader's expectations and the way he or she may construct the significance of the passage is subverted or made problematic. Secondly, the foregrounding of 'things' or 'background' does not allow the reader to read character solely in terms of the human, other characters, or 'people'. But neither is s/he allowed to read the physical world of 'things' merely as personifications of mood or character. Although the room is later presented as haven (II, 321), or cell (III, 31), beautiful or bleak, according to Miriam's projections, the facticity, the 'thinginess' of the six-page description at the beginning of *The Tunnel*, serves to remind the reader of the room's material existence, that things or objects exist independently of human appetites and desires.

Another effect achieved by the technique here is to make the point that Miriam is in the room, the room is in the house, and the house is in London – and indeed that London is a city in a wider world. Like the list in Stephen Dedalus's geography book in *A Portrait of the Artist as a Young Man*, ('Stephen Dedalus, Class of Elements, Clongowes Wood School, Sallins, County Kildare, Ireland, Europe, The World, The Universe') it situates the woman in the wider world. Richardson extends the figure of the house, traditionally used to represent a woman's social and psychic existence, to the city; her use of the larger figure (the city) in conjunction with the smaller figures of rooms and houses makes possible a more mobile and extensive set of figures: streets, intersections and city zones as well as walls, doors and windows. In this way, the public and private realms are brought into a new textual relation, and the syntagmatic nature of the spatial imagery allows the reader to map the psychic and social as contiguous, not alternative orders.

Thus the volumes between *The Tunnel* and *Clear Horizon* repeatedly present Miriam's exits and entrances from house to street and back again; walking and cycling through the streets, going to lectures, visiting friends and restaurants. Like the

figures in Gwen John's paintings, Miriam is continually
positioned in relation to doors and windows, looking outwards,
towards something not in the room. This move from interior
to exterior in the text, taking the heroine out of 'the home'
and on to the streets of London, corresponds to an actual
enlargement in women's sphere of movement during the
period 1896–1908. Improvements in the policing and lighting
of central London, the extension of the underground system,
bicycles and loosening codes of respectability, meant greater
freedom for the middle-class woman than ever before. The
gain is registered in Miriam's image of the city as an extended
house, of Londoners,

> going about happy, the minute they were out of their houses,
> looking at nothing and feeling everything, like people wandering
> happily from room to room in a well-known house. . . . (II, 156)

In the nineteenth-century novel, while the male characters
might enjoy the freedom of the streets, the heroine's freedom
from the codes and conventions of 'the home', is usually
represented by excursions into 'nature', to the countryside.
The streets might be free to men and prostitutes, but for the
middle-class woman they represent either danger or disgrace;
only at home was she safe from 'all injury. . .terror, doubt and
division' in Ruskin's phrase.

In *Pilgrimage*, women's new freedoms at the turn of the
century are imaged as both a room of her own *and* freedom
of the streets, as if to stress the interrelation between the
struggle for mental and physical 'space'. The room provides
the solitude necessary for Miriam's self-realisation, the city a
sense of community in which to develop a new social identity.
The difficulties of achieving either (let alone both) are fully
documented in this text, and the spatial movements – all those
exits and entrances – work, in my reading, to represent the
necessary links between them. The effect of this imagery is
cumulative and in a text of such length there are many
individual passages which contribute to its overall significance,
but the following extract from *Interim* will serve as an example
of Richardson's method, its pleasures and its problems.

> She strolled to the window, finding renewal in the familiar creaking
> of her floor in the house, here. . . . She went back across the happy
> creaking and turned out the gas and came again to the window.

The sky was dark enough to show a brilliant star; here and there in the darkness of the opposite housefronts was an oblong of golden light. The faint blue light coming up from the street lit up the outer edges of the grey stone window-sills. The air under the wooden roof of the window space was almost as close as it was under the immense height of upper coolness. . . . Down at the end of the road were the lamplit green trees; plane-tree shadows on the narrow pavement. She put on her hat in the dark.

Crossing the roadway to reach the narrow strip of pavement running along under the trees she saw single dark figures standing at intervals against the brilliant lamplit green and swerved back to the wide pavement. She had forgotten they would be there. They stood like sentinels. . . . Behind them the lamplit green flared feverishly. . . . In the shadow of St Pancras Church there were others, small and black in a desert. . .lost quickly in the great shadow where the passers-by moved swiftly through from light to light. Out in the Euston Road along the pavements shadowed by trees and left in darkness by the high spindling shaded candles of the lamps along the centre of the roadway, they came walking, a foreign walk, steadily slow and wavy and expressive, here and there amongst the expressionless forms of the London wayfarers. The high stone entrance of Euston Station shone white across the way. Anyone can go into a station. Within the entrance gravelled darkness opened out on either side. Silence all round and ahead, where silent buildings had here and there a lit window. Where was the station? Immense London darkness and stillness alone and deserted like a country place at night, just beyond the noises of the Euston Road. A murder might happen here. The cry of an engine sounded, muffled and far away. Just ahead in the centre of the approaching wide mass of building was a wide dimly lit stone archway. The rattle of a hansom sounded from an open space beyond. Its light appeared swaying swiftly forward and lit the archway. The hansom bowled through in startling silence, nothing but the jingle and dumb leathery rattle of the harness, and passed, the plonking of the horse's hoofs and the swift slur of the wheels sounding out again in the open space. The archway had little side pathways for passengers roofed by small arching extensions of the central arch. . .*indiarubber*. . .pavement to muffle. . .the building was an hotel; Edwards's daylight Family Hotel. . .expensive people lodging just above the arch, travelling, coming to London, going away from London, with no thought of the dark secret neighbourhood. (II, 409–10)

How is this to be read? As a description of an evening walk? As an exercise in the 'reality effect' where the detail is designed to ensure the reader will accept the world alluded to here as 'real'? Neither explanation seems adequate for the complex effects produced here. It seems too long as a realistic description, and too obscure to contribute to 'the reality effect'. Again, Richardson's mode of writing baffles interpretation even as it invites it. It draws attention to itself as *writing*, the elaborate series of repetitions, of alliteration and assonance, the contrasting motifs (of light and dark, sound and silence, etc.) are more immediately striking than the scene to which these refer. As writing it actively solicits the collaboration of the reader and I would here like to fall headlong into the interpretive trap, so seductively set up in this passage, by reading it in terms of 'space for women'.

At the time of writing *Interim* (1919), Dorothy Richardson had not yet begun her monthly columns in the film journal *Close-Up*, but the grammar of her visual images, the way they are put together, might well be called cinematic. The first paragraph, for example, opens with a tracking shot which moves from Miriam ('She') to the window and what she can see through it (the sky, housefronts, the lamplit green trees), then back to her putting on her hat in the dark. Her exit from the house is edited out, and the next paragraph cuts to her crossing the roadway. From here on, despite the third-person, the 'point-of-view' is Miriam's as if she is a hand-held camera seeing 'Just ahead. . .the approaching wide mass of building'. What she sees, once outside the house, are 'single dark figures' standing in the shadows. Referred to only as 'they', the identity of these figures is left uncertain; the reader is told that they cause her to swerve 'back to the wide pavement', that 'she had forgotten they would be there', and that they stood 'like sentinels', but not who or what 'they' are. Only later in the paragraph are these figures, found in the streets and squares near Euston Station and sheltering in the shadows of the Blakean church, characterised by their walk – 'steadily slow and wavy and expressive'. The reader's suppositions are here confirmed. But finding a referent for the pronoun 'they', one still has to find a 'meaning' for the referent. The obliquely presented prostitutes may represent Miriam's linguistic inhibitions, but they also present some of the problems of reading and writing.

Do the prostitutes mark, for example, the limits to Miriam's freedom, the point that she must stick to the 'wide pavements' if she is not to mingle with women who earn their living on the streets? Described as standing 'like sentinels', they suggest the boundaries between the respectable, who stay in 'Edwards's daylight Family Hotel', and those who stand or are cast into the darkness outside it. (Miriam's subsequent thought that 'murder might happen here' may also remind the reader of the multiple murders of prostitutes in Whitechapel only a decade before.[13]) In Victorian melodrama 'they' might signify the ultimate danger that may befall a middle-class woman, in medical terms they may represent 'the great scourge' of venereal disease, while in Mayhew's account 'they' might be some of the third and lowest class of the estimated 80,000 prostitutes in London (Mayhew, 1950: 32). To take possession of the space offered by the streets, Miriam must encounter its existing occupants; it is not virgin territory to be conquered, one might say, but, like the language that Richardson must employ, it is territory always already occupied. The 'dark figures' I would argue, represent both the heroine's sexual fears *and* the social realities which surround her, but beyond that, 'they' exemplify the problems for a woman writing about women's sexuality, the problem of figuration.

Miriam is driven forth on her walk by a restiveness which, it is suggested, is both sexual and literary: reading in her room, she has become dissatisfied with 'the language of ideas', with adjectives which do not describe but are 'opinions' and she muses over male writing with the question 'Why do men write books?' (II, 407). That question, together with its silent correlative, 'Why do women?' is planted in the reader's mind before the walk is described. To use the existing names like 'prostitutes' would be for Richardson to fall into existing categorisations, male definitions of women as pure and impure, the respectable and the fallen, etc. To escape the 'language of [male] ideas', the writer must make a more devious and indirect use of language. And this, I think, to go back to my starting point, is what the writing in this passage is about: to write about 'sexuality' and 'prostitution' in ways which produce the difference of view, produce a new figuration. It is a gender-motivated form of defamiliarisation.

Using a cityscape rather than the landscape employed by Charlotte Brontë or George Eliot, the street descriptions chart

the various outlets for female sexuality. At the most obvious
level, the wide and narrow pavements and paths signify that
a woman must choose her path with care and that Miriam, in
taking to the streets, is transgressing class and gender
proprieties which place her at risk. The intersecting roads, well
or badly lit, the broad and narrow paths, the lit windows and
open spaces, operate as an extended metaphor for the different
sexual and social options for the woman of the period. The
central arch lit by the hansom and the 'jingle and dumb
leathery rattle of the harness', lead to sexuality within the
family (signified by Edwards's *Family* Hotel), but the arch has
little side pathways – 'small arching extensions of the central
arch'. The architectural detail used here seems to posit
an interconnection between the family and prostitution,
suggesting that the latter is an extension of the former. The
word *'indiarubber'* (italicised to signal a delayed recognition but
suggestive, in the context, of the new forms of contraception)
introduces other perturbing questions: is the hansom, like
Woolf's image of the taxi in *A Room Of One's Own*, an image
of men and women's relationship? Does the 'pavement to
muffle' imply, for example, that the entrance to Edwards's
Family Hotel muffles the wheels of other kinds of sexuality?
Is it the coming of new technology ('indiarubber') which allows
one to hear the 'rattle of the harness' sounding out 'in the
open space'? Or is it simply that the courtyard of the hotel, as
Miriam realises, must be rubber coated to lessen the noise of
the horses' hoofs – like that of the Savoy Hotel?[14]

There are no exact equivalences or clear-cut symbols in the
passage, only the silent film image of the hansom and a series
of suggestive details to incite the reader to interpretation. By
the end of this section, in a passage not cited here, Miriam, it
is implied, has a new consciousness of her situation as a
woman: 'Waiting outside was the walk back through the
various darkness, the indiarubber pathway. . .knowing her
way' (II, 410). For the character, if not for the reader, her voyage
out into the night-time city has been enlightening. The passage
can be linked back to an earlier one in *The Tunnel* where
Miriam is herself mistaken for a prostitute (II, 96), and forwards
to the next chapter of *Interim* where the heroine learns that a
respectable doctor 'had made up his mind to speak' (II, 432),

was about to propose marriage, but was deterred by reports of her street outings with the disreputable and aptly named Mendizabal. The 'plot' would thus confirm what has been implied in this descriptive passage: that the world like the streets is so arranged that the heroine's freedom to explore may cause her to forfeit the safety and security of bourgeois marriage. Miriam's later comment on London 'No one in the world could oust this mighty lover' (III, 272) derives much of its significance directly and indirectly from the spatial metonymies set up in the *Interim* passage. Thus the problem, it seems to me, is not that the details are not 'significant' or cannot be made to signify, but that, as with Joyce or Woolf herself, so much depends on the collaborative reader.

Street haunting

Woolf herself made extensive use of London as a setting in both *Night and Day* (1919) and *Mrs Dalloway* (1925) but her essay on London entitled 'Street haunting: a London adventure' was not written until 1930, after the publication of the first nine volumes of *Pilgrimage*. Describing a walk across London on the pretext of buying a pencil, the essay echoes many of Richardson's most characteristic points about the city.

It presents for example the social heterogeneity of the city, the variety of human contacts, in descriptions of the shop-girl, the dwarf, the good citizen, the two men under a lamppost discussing a Newmarket wire and 'the stout lady tightly swathed in shiny sealskin' (Woolf, 1947: 22). Like Richardson, Woolf stresses the anonymity that a large city may offer the woman *flâneur*, the point that 'the anonymity of the crowd provides an asylum for the person on the margins of society' (Woolf, 1985: 40). In *Pilgrimage* Miriam becomes 'not a woman but a Londoner' (III, 272) while for Woolf:

> We are no longer quite ourselves. . .we shed the self our friends know us by and become part of that vast republican army of anonymous trampers. . . .(Woolf, 1947: 19)

She also presents the city stroller as a fragmented self:

> Am I here, or am I there? Or is the true self neither this nor that, neither here nor there, but something so varied and wandering. . . .(Woolf, 1947: 24)

Both writers celebrate the city by a detailed evocation of 'the fugitive, the random, the contingent' but whereas Richardson accumulates detail for the reader to give meaning to, Woolf offers the reader more in the way of interpreting/narrativising her details.

> But this is London, we are reminded; high among the bare trees are hung oblong frames of reddish yellow light – windows; there are points of brilliance burning steadily like low stars – lamps: this empty ground. . .is only a London square, set about by offices and houses where at this hour fierce lights burn over maps, over documents, over desks where clerks sit turning with wetted forefinger the files of endless correspondences; or more suffusedly the firelight wavers and the lamplight falls on the privacy of some drawing-room, its easy chairs, its papers, its china, its inlaid table, and the figure of a woman, accurately measuring out the precise number of spoons of tea which – She looks at the door as if she heard a ring downstairs and somebody asking, is she in?
> But here we must stop peremptorily. (Woolf, 1985: 40)

Woolf uses a plenitude of detail to present the exterior and interior spaces of the city and the figure of the woman within it doing what she, the invisible *flâneuse*, has escaped from: tea-making, waiting for social calls. The material, the situation of 'street haunting' is in many respects similar to that used in the different chapters of *Pilgrimage*, but the method is different. Richardson's method, according to Woolf,

> demands attention, as a door whose handle we wrench ineffectively calls our attention to the fact that it is locked. (Woolf, 1979: 188)

Woolf's own method, to use the same metaphor, is more like a door with a handle on which the word TURN is written in embossed characters. The door may open but our attention and interest is called to the mechanism, the device by which the opening is achieved. Here we are offered a story about a woman seen from the street, but the teasing refusal to continue with the story signals that what matters is the story-making not the story. For what the passage dramatises is the need to interpret, to make up stories about what is seen. It *enacts* the process whereby details are made significant. In many ways one might see Woolf's essay as an ironical rewriting of

Richardson's London adventure, an essay at an alternative method. Woolf, Richardson and Katherine Mansfield all celebrate the city in their different ways, but a study of their use of space suggests that it is Richardson rather than Mansfield who is Woolf's chief rival and inspiration.

In *Pilgrimage* the quality and quantity of the spatial imagery varies from novel to novel, nevertheless one can trace its interlocking patterns running like filigree across the sequence. 'Space' and 'spaciousness' are terms used throughout *Pilgrimage* to refer to the character's aspirations, her desire for growth or self-realisation. Her fears of 'engulfment' or confinement on the other hand are registered as 'enclosure', closed doors or windows, or encroaching walls. 'Walls. What *are* walls?' (II, 336) she asks at one point. Walls, like other spatial elements are never one thing. At defensive moments, walls may represent the safety or protectiveness of the 'maison natale';[15] at other points, when she is in love with Shatov (III, 87) or exhilarated at the thought of pregnancy, her expanding consciousness takes her 'Up in the clouds' (IV, 281) beyond the walls of her now breached body and in contact with the 'vibrating particles of light' (IV, 282).

Increasingly, in the middle and later volumes, the heroine's speech is registered in the same spatial imagery used by her narrator, thus intensifying the effect. In *The Trap* Miriam's judgement on a friend, 'She had no back premises' (III, 406) uses an image based on the social divisions of the Victorian household to characterise the limitations of the woman whose rooms she shares. In this way Miss Holland's lack of inner life is economically linked to the system of which she is a product. Miriam's sense of the differences between masculine and feminine consciousness are stated in similar terms: 'One *moment* of my consciousness is wider and deeper than his has been the *whole* of his life' (IV, 132). Like the earlier heroine Jane Eyre, looking out over the battlements of Thornfield, Miriam expresses her sexual and social longings, her 'power of vision' in spatial terms. When, in the later novels, she moves away from the Fabians and the 'intermittent feminism' of her earlier life towards a mystical path, this too is expressed in terms of her conviction that: 'There's more space within, than without' (IV, 167). And as Miriam turns at the end of *March*

Moonlight from a religious vocation to writing, it is the 'inner vastness' that she sets out to record.

'London' and its streets and buildings changes its meaning from text to text. Street scenes are used to present her growing love for Michael Shatov 'the bliss of post offices' in *Deadlock* and her parting from Hypo Wilson in *Clear Horizon*. Specific areas of the city may be associated with specific events, as is 'Teetgens Teas' street with her mother's suicide, or with specific states of mind. The mean streets of Holloway, for example, stand in Miriam's mind for confinement, the constrictions in her life, whereas the shabby spacious eighteenth-century houses of Bloomsbury are consistently linked to her sense of possibilities. Certain roads and streets are paralleled with particular emotional tracks along which her thoughts and feelings run: rage, pleasure, hope and despair. She learns to recognise, if not to avoid, particular emotional pathways as so many dead-end streets. The city and its constructions become a figure for the myriad 'I ams' of the woman 'Mir-i-am' and its thousand and one streets represent the *mille tre* women that she contains. Its 'dark secret neighbourhoods' and Family Hotels, its network of intersecting streets are full, like the heroine's mind, of past history, present choices and future perspectives. In 'the jumble of a great metropolis' (Freud, 1961: 70) Richardson finds a figure sufficiently complex and various to textualise 'the history of a woman's life'.

But 'London' in the text is not just a means to project the social situation of a woman, it operates as another kind of scene, *eine andere Schauplatz* , as a figuration of a woman's fantasies: her fantasy, for example, of an ideal environment in which the conflicts and divisions of everyday life no longer exist, a place where one might return to an imaginary unity:

> tonight the spirit of London came to meet her on the verge. Nothing in life could be sweeter than this welcoming – a cup held brimming to her lips, and inexhaustible. What lover did she want? No one in the world would oust this mighty lover, always receiving her back without words, engulfing and leaving her untouched, liberated and expanding to the whole range of her being. (III, 272)

'London. . .this mighty lover' appears not just as an alternative to various male suitors, but as an image of a different kind of time or space: the maternal body. A nurturing space, full of 'the sound of the sea' (I, 421), 'engulfing her and leaving her untouched', it allows her to exist in an anonymous ungendered state ('not a woman but a Londoner'), offering her a blissful enjoyment of its riches and 'an oblivion deeper than sleep. . .within the vast surrounding presence' (III, 272). London, in other words, serves to register the importance of fantasy in psychic life as well as a social critique of women's conditions of existence. It may be that the fascination with the spatial, in Richardson, Woolf and other women writers like Colette and Rhys, is an attempt to signify this lost world, the somewhere beyond 'a place in linear time as the time of project and history' which 'is experienced as extra-subjective time, cosmic time, [and can] occasion vertiginous visions and unnameable *jouissance*' (Kristeva, 1986: 191)

City with a difference

In contrast to many male writings of the same period, *Pilgrimage* uses London, the city, primarily as a positive image. Whereas in canonical English modernism, with the notable exception of Joyce, the city is a wasteland, the site of usury, a place of debilitating decadence or of metaphysical evil, in Richardson's text it is compared to a 'prairie' (II, 156), a 'mighty lover' (III, 272), it is a celestial city with 'pavements of heaven' (I, 416) and a plenitude of possibilities. There is little hankering after an organic countryside, even as an escape from the economic and social problems so vividly depicted. Why, one might ask, does Richardson in *Pilgrimage* (and Woolf in *Mrs Dalloway*) celebrate the city in ways most of their male contemporaries do not? Or why, to put the question the other way round, does it figure so negatively in much male writing?

Pilgrimages in search of the past had become a feature of literary culture in the late Victorian/Edwardian period, in William Morris's late writings, in Gissing, Forster, Masterman, Belloc and others. Critiques of industrial capitalism and its effects and values – from right, left and centre – took the city as a symbolic target. As Raymond Williams[16] and others have argued, idealisation of the countryside has a long history, but at the turn of the century this anti-urbanism played a key role in the construction of the idea of 'Englishness', the English way of life, the English character. In brief, the best of English traditions was deemed to be in the past and the past was to be found in the countryside. The city stood for change, the country for continuity, stability and permanence. As Masterman put it in *The Condition of England* (1909): 'The life of old England is the life of the village' or as the journalist Philip Gibbs later claimed:

> England is not to be judged only by the monstrous ant heap called London. . . . There is still the English countryside where life goes on traditionally in old farmsteads.

This construction had, of course, crucial effects, well charted elsewhere, on architecture, on demographic movements and on the formation of the national cultural identity.

Raymond Williams in his discussion of these issues in *The Country and the City*, does not mention Richardson but singles out Wells as the writer of the period who, partly for class reasons, most forcefully challenges this construction. He then moves on to discuss London as the city of light, in the physical sense of its new street lighting (Williams, 1973: 227–30). In *Pilgrimage*, London is a city of light in another sense, a place of work and freedom, of experience and education for the pilgrim who wanders its carnival streets. Miriam moves from suburban home to central London, where the bulk of the novels are set, and significantly it is to London that she returns at the end of the last novel, *March Moonlight*, to continue her journey in writing.

What motivates *this* difference of view? Both class and gender – but gender specifically. Miriam *is* capable of seeing London in terms of class but this is rare. Watching the Bank Holiday crowds she feels

> The certainty that this wild tumult of people is the reality and the rest a sham. I almost feared to look at them lest they see me wondering *why* they go back. Why they don't know their power and end the system that holds them. (III, 501–2)

The London she loves is built, she recognises here, on the labour of these 'toiling' invisible masses of people. The carnival scene makes them, for a day, visible as a force and triggers a Shelleyan recognition ('Ye are many, they are few'). Against her vision of these 'rampant multitudes' (III, 502) she conjures up the image of the poet Yeats reading his poetry to a green-robed woman. At this moment they seem,

> Irrelevant and insecure. As if they might topple. Ought to topple. Ought to listen and topple down. (III, 502–3)

It is a moment of split consciousness, emphasised by the shifts between first- and third-person. Miriam identifies both with the position of the privileged poet but also with 'all those people who keep London what it is to me' (III, 502).

In gender terms Miriam's own shifting class position alerts her to the fact that gender conventions are not 'natural' or given but vary according to class or the class fragment a woman belongs to – it may, for example, be a feminine mark of pride for an upper middle-class girl to profess ignorance of cookery, but not so for a teacher, or clerical worker. Her gender position on the other hand, teaches her that a countryside governed by rigid sexual codes ('the enclosed outlook from the Roscorlas') can never be paradisiacal for a woman.

If there is very little sense generated in the novel-sequence of a past spoilt or compromised by urbanism, it may be for the very basic reason that the 'English way of life' was already spoilt for the woman heroine. The conservatism of the English past, the text indicates, meant restriction, dependence, imprisonment, whereas London is imaged as positive, enabling – 'always receiving her back, engulfing and leaving her untouched, liberated and expanding to the whole range of her being' (III, 272). As a woman, both inside and outside the culture represented by the metropolitan city, her possession of this 'mighty lover' can never be secure. As Virginia Woolf later put it, with due significance, in *A Room Of One's Own*,

> if one is a woman one is often surprised by a sudden splitting off of consciousness, say in walking down Whitehall when from being the natural inheritor of that civilisation, she becomes, on the contrary, outside of it, alien and critical. (Woolf, 1929: 96)

Nevertheless, as a 'batteur de pavé' (II, 392), London is the only community open to this *déclassée* woman and she plants her bean-rows on its grey pavements with neo-romantic effusions of gratitude. So in this respect too, Richardson in *Pilgrimage* looks at the dominant construction of the city, and the ideology of 'Englishness' forged from it in the early twentieth century, with 'the eyes of a stranger'.

Chapter Four

The enigma of woman

It is impossible to dissociate the questions of art, style and truth from the question of the woman. Nevertheless the question 'what is woman?' is itself suspended by the simple formulation of their common problematic. One can no longer seek her, no more than one could search for woman's femininity or female sexuality. And she is certainly not to be found in any of the familiar modes of concept or knowledge. Yet it is impossible to resist looking for her.

(Derrida, 1979: 71)

Shadows were there. The shadow of Nietzsche, the problem of free-love, the challenge of Weiniger [*sic*], the triple tangle of art, sex, and religion. (III, 482)

Early reviewers, whether sympathetic or hostile, were quick to recognise both the feminist element and the formal innovations of Richardson's novel. The relation between the feminism and the modernism of the text, although noted by reviewers such as Woolf and Mansfield was not, however, seriously pursued. Yet the connections between the two elements are vital and this chapter will attempt to explore the ways in which the question of woman is tied to the question of 'art, style and truth' in *Pilgrimage*.

For Richardson one question led to another, and her attempts to untangle the question of woman led not only to stylistic change, but to the unravelling of her whole intellectual fabric. The 'shadow of Nietzsche', referred to by Miriam above, is not, I think, the shadow of his misogyny, but the shadow cast by his reflections upon language, truth and sexuality. In her review of Orage's book on Nietzsche in *The Open Road* in 1907, Richardson argues against the English reading of Nietzsche as a 'decadent monster', urging the reader to make direct contact with the writings of this 'luminous and tender' philosopher. The distrust of 'system', truth and language, and the conception of love as 'beyond good and evil' in the novel are directly linked to the German philosopher's work and *Pilgrimage* may be read as a (woman's) response to Nietzsche.

Pilgrimage and the New Woman

Richardson's novel-sequence, as numerous critics have noted, offers a powerful critique of masculine and feminine roles at the end of the nineteenth and the beginning of the twentieth century. If it did no more than that, it would constitute only a late flowering of the 'New Woman' fiction produced in the 1890s – an assemblage of points made by Egerton, Grand, Mona Caird and others.[1] Richardson could certainly be said to start from the formulations of these earlier writers and George Egerton's statement about her writing is relevant to Richardson's project in *Pilgrimage*:

> I realised that in literature, everything had been better done by a man than woman could have hoped to emulate. There was only one small plot left to tell: the *terra incognita* of herself, as she knew herself to be, not as man liked to imagine her – in a word to give herself away, as man had given himself away in his writings.[2]

A writer of short stories, Egerton describes this *terra incognita* as a *supplement* to the existing world of literature, but with Dorothy Richardson the 'small plot' becomes an enormous field of enquiry, one which for her transforms the whole map of writing. The difference is that for Richardson rewriting 'woman' meant rewriting the world.

Egerton's claim that the woman writer will 'give herself away' ('as man had given himself away in his writings') is again relevant. What Egerton's writing gives (away) is an essentialist view of a 'natural' woman, as if inside the constrictive clothing imposed by patriarchal England, there is a 'real' woman struggling to get out. With a new Ibsen-ish realism, her writing focuses on the inner life of her feminine characters, on 'the untamed primitive savage temperament that lurks in the mildest, best woman'.[3] Locating her feminine characters in the 'eternal wildness' of nature, rather than in Ruskin's sacred temple of culture, the 'natural' or God-given elements are posed in direct opposition to the social or man-made: 'In one word, the untrue feminine is of man's making, whilst the strong, the natural, the true womanly is of God's making'.[4] In this formulation one definition of 'woman' is replaced by another. The *terra incognita* becomes a *terra firma*, named and settled, as it were.

The protagonist of *Pilgrimage* also denigrates 'the untrue feminine' and idealises 'the true womanly', but in my reading of the text, these are Miriam's 'shadows'. Her dilemmas with the category 'woman' are *exhibited* through the writing, not endorsed. Her views on woman, which shift from denigration to idealisation, from seeing her in terms of 'lack' or 'plenitude', are presented as cultural and psychic fantasies – posed as part of the problem and not, I think, as the solution. In this respect my reading differs from that of Showalter and DuPlessis who seem to assume that *Pilgrimage*, like *Keynotes*, offers a celebration of 'the true womanly'. Reading *Pilgrimage* as autobiography, they tend to treat Miriam/Richardson/*Pilgrimage* as identical, as offering one and the same position.[5] But although Richardson, in many reviews and articles (see 'Das Ewig-Weibliche') makes statements on women very close to those of her protagonist, her insistence elsewhere that *Pilgrimage* is 'fiction' not autobiography, and her rage with reviewers who confused her with her character,[6] mark the importance of the distinction for the writer. For the reader, the collapse of protagonist, 'author' and text into a single position radically simplifies what *Pilgrimage* has to say on 'the triple tangle of art, sex and religion', and the ways in which it suspends Derrida's (and Nietzsche's) question 'what is woman?' within a new problematic.

For one thing, the blurring of the character/author distinction may obscure the point that *Pilgrimage* is a *historical novel* in which the earlier period is read through the new discourses about women and femininity produced after the First World

War – discourses which were not available to Miriam, nor to Egerton and earlier women writers. Richardson reads 'the past' of her heroine (the 1890s to 1912) from different vantage points (the 1920s, 1930s and later) and this itself, as Miriam's comment at the end of the sequence reminds the reader, makes a difference:

> While I write. . .The whole of what is called 'the past' is with me, seen anew, vividly. No, Schiller, the past does not stand 'being still'. It moves, growing with one's growth. (IV, 657)

The past can only be known through the present, it is constantly reread, reinterpreted through the present. But as the novels were written over a period spanning from 1912 to 1957, there is no fixed historical vantage point either – the only 'present' is the moment of writing (or reading) which like the 'the past' it becomes can always be 'seen anew'. Certain incidents are presented very differently at different moments in the sequence with important effects. Compare, for example, the account of the Ted/Max incident in *Backwater* (I, 218–25) (1916) with that given in *March Moonlight* (IV, 644–5) (1967). The narrative presents two very different versions of why Miriam did not marry 'Ted', but the later version has no more authority than the earlier. The meaning of the incident is left undecided. Whatever the autobiographical sources of the material therefore, there is no steady progression towards the 'truth', no conception of the past *or* present as fixed or fixing meaning. The moment of interpretation in writing/reading provides only one (transitory) point among others.

The blurring of character/text may obscure another point about Richardson's method: that while the narrator is allowed to present only the *consciousness*[7] of the protagonist, the text represents the *unconscious* forces working within and *through* that consciousness. The words on the page (the representation of consciousness) are supplemented by a range of typographical devices: ellipses, italics, segmented passages, gaps and spaces in the text. These devices represent the repressions and gaps in consciousness, or that which is left unsaid or is unsayable. Miriam frequently opposes silence to speech, emphasising 'the quality of the in-between silences' (III, 389) as a source of meaning. And in the text there are actually *printed silences* to register the activities of the unconscious which neither speech nor writing can reach. These blank spaces signal, more eloquently than any words, the blind spots of language and consciousness.

Pilgrimage by methods such as these takes the questions raised by New Woman fiction onto new ground, and in doing so changes the nature of the questions. First, it presents femininity not as a matter of biology or essence, but *as a position to be occupied,* and the uncertainties of sexual identity are inserted into a general set of questions about the subject and sexuality. Secondly, Miriam's development as a woman is explored in relation to 'family romance', – how, for example, her fantasies of the mother govern her relationships with women (and men) in adult life. Thirdly, perhaps most significantly, *Pilgrimage* uses existing representations of 'woman' to consider the nature and limitations of those representations and, more generally, to comment on representation as a process. What the writing of *Pilgrimage* 'gives away' is the impossibility of arriving at any stable definition of 'woman', of dissociating, as Derrida puts it, 'the questions of art, style and truth from the question of the woman'.

Femininity as masquerade

The first three novels of *Pilgrimage,* published during the First World War, introduce the gender theme via a point of change in the protagonist's situation: Miriam leaving home. Her entry into the world outside the family forces her to confront the gap between her own sense of gender identity and the world's definition of her as 'woman'. It motivates a series of reflections on the relation between the (masculine) subject position taken up and the (female) body she inhabits. Within a family of four daughters, unable to accept 'her own disappointing birth as the third girl' (I, 32) the protagonist is identified and identifies herself with the father, with a masculine position. Her independence, strength and cleverness, culturally defined as masculine, are all linked to her missed 'appointment' as the son of the family – a family romance in which other family members apparently collude:

Pater knew how hateful all the world of women were and despised
them. He never included her with them; or only sometimes when
she pretended, or he didn't understand. . . . (I, 22)

Her mother and sisters, while accepting their own feminine
positions, appear to support Miriam's masculine pretensions
by recognising her difference from themselves in similar terms,
as a gender difference. In her mother's telling phrase: 'You
ought to be a man, Mimmy' (I, 193).

Repudiating the feminine within herself and identifying
with her father's position of intellectual superiority over her
'small and resourceless' mother (I, 193), 'Mimmy' reiterates
whenever possible his hostile and contemptuous views of
women. But although she begins from his clear-cut division
between men and women, her own uneasy position straddling
that divide brings with it a difference of view. Unlike her
father who assumes that feminine behaviour stems from
women's 'nature', Miriam perceives women as constantly
'pretending', acting, playing a part, especially in the presence
of men. In *Pointed Roofs*, even the schoolgirls in Hanover seem
to change in male company:

It frightened and disgusted her to see that all the girls seemed to
be sitting up and. . .being bright. . .affected. She could hardly
believe it. She flushed with shame. . . . Fast, horrid. . .perfect
strangers. . .it spoilt everything. Sitting up like that grimacing. . . .
(I, 155–6)

The strength of her conscious reaction (incredulity, disgust,
shame) is reported without comment by the narrator but the
ellipses mark a level of activity not represented in the account.
They emphasize not only the intensity of her reaction but a
certain disparity between cause and effect, a missing link
between the perception and the reaction. The device alerts the
reader to areas of repression in Miriam's consciousness, what
the 17-year-old girl is not conscious of in her motivation and
it invites the reader to pose questions about the content of
this. Is, for example, her repudiation of a particular mode of
feminine behaviour a screen for another kind of disavowal?
Or her 'shame' at evidence of others' sexual interest evidence
of her own? However read, the ellipses make the point, a point
about form, that these 'silences' supplement the representation
of subjectivity in language; they indicate what can never quite

be known, but never quite be *not* known, by the subject in question.

The passage cited above is juxtaposed with one in which Miriam, in a romantic daydream, stares fixedly at a male teacher until she notices the eyes of the headmistress upon her: 'she read there a disgust and loathing such as she had never seen' (I, 157). Fräulein Pfaff's 'disgust' is the mirror of Miriam's in the previous scene, what she had felt but 'never seen', and the doubling of the two narrative incidents underlines the comparison between the two characters. As the narrative has already established, part of the Fräulein's professional role, as head of school, is to discipline and deny the expression of sexuality in her charges. Miriam, one might say, is involved in a similar enterprise, the government of her own unruly libidinal 'charges'. Again, the position of the heroine and the narrative could in no sense be called identical here, since the text produces ('gives away') a knowledge of Miriam and her subjectivity not available to the character. It opens it up to the reader's collaboration.

The question of feminine identity as a form of masquerade is further developed in the next two novels, *Backwater* and *Honeycomb*. Miriam's position is initially based on a rejection of feminine role-playing as a shameful travesty of true womanliness performed by *some* women, but when both her mother and sisters insist that 'we're all different when there are men about to when we're by ourselves. We all make eyes, in a way' (I, 302) she becomes conscious of a new set of problems: that she too changes under the male gaze, that 'men admire them for looking. . .like that' (I, 301), that she is unable to define 'woman' except in relation to their play-acting or masquerade. In her apprenticeship to the role of woman, Miriam reaches a point of recognition described by Joan Riviere, that under the male gaze women change, they perform the role of – 'woman'. She begins to fear that unless she too disguises her masculine identifications under a masquerade of womanliness, she can never be a 'woman':

> Womanliness therefore could be assumed and worn as a mask, both to hide the possession of masculinity and to avert the reprisals expected if she were found to possess it – much as a thief will turn out his pockets and ask to be searched to prove that he has

not the stolen goods. The reader may now ask how I define
womanliness or where I draw the line between genuine womanliness and the masquerade. My suggestion is not, however that
there is any such difference, whether radical or superficial, *they
are the same thing.*[8] (My italics)

In Riviere's case-history, womanliness as a masquerade is
used by an intellectual woman who does not accept 'the fact
of castration' but rather than making overt 'her wish or claim
to be a man' seeks to disguise it behind a 'veil' of femininity.
The protagonist in *Pilgrimage* is an intellectual woman who
finds it difficult to adopt this strategy, finds it easier indeed to
make her claims to the masculine position 'overt'. Nevertheless,
when she does attempt to put herself in the feminine position,
her attempts produce some brilliant observations on feminine
identity and the operations of the 'masquerade'. In *Backwater*,
Miriam literally dons a veil in an attempt to hide her 'difference'
from the womanly woman, to hide her masculine identifications
behind the protective cover of spotted net veiling (I, 266).
Behind this warm and comforting veil she resolves to practise
various penitential rituals 'until she had grown like those
women who were called blessed' (I, 267). To become a woman
'called blessed' for Miriam at this stage is to become a religious
womanly woman desired by men, and thus to be rescued from
a life she fears: poverty and drudgery as an unmarried teacher,
'feeling ill and sad, having a yellow face and faded hair and
not enough saved to live on when she was too old to work'
(I, 274). The social and economic reasons for the masquerade
are clear and compelling ones, but even so the heroine is
unable to sustain it. There are equally compelling reasons, it
seems, which drive her away from an effective assumption of
the feminine position.

In *The Tunnel*, for example, she finds an opportunity to
assume the part of 'a very religious, very womanly woman,
the ideal wife and mother' (II, 27) playing Mendelssohn's
'Songs Without Words' to a Byronic admirer called Mr
Tremayne. Entering into the fantasy, she gives an excellent
performance of both the piece and role:

> It was such an easy part to play. She could go on playing it to the
> end of her life, if he went on in business and made enough money,
> being a 'gracious silence', taking an interest in his affairs, ordering

> things well, quietly training the servants, never losing her temper
> or raising her voice, making home a sanctuary of rest and
> refinement and religious aspiration, going to church. . . . She felt
> all these things expressing themselves in her bearing. At the end
> of her piece she was touched to the heart by the look of adoration
> in his eyes, the innocent youthfulness shining through his face. . . .
> (II, 27)

At the end of the piece, however, she abandons her role as
one of Ruskin's queens, and sails forth into a piece by
Beethoven playing with the energy and abandon required by
'the great truth' of the music. At the end of *this* performance,

> She got up, charged to the fingertips with a glow that transfigured
> all the inanimate things in the room. The party was wrecked. . .a
> young lady who banged the piano till her hair nearly came
> down. . . . Mr. Tremayne had heard nothing but noise. . . . His
> eyes smiled, and his uneasy mouth felt for compliments. (II, 28)

Miriam makes a spectacle of herself. She puts off the veil of
femininity (*'le voile tombe'*) and unmasks herself as a phallic
woman who refuses to play the role of 'woman' for man. She
would, as the scene neatly encapsulates, rather play the piano
than the masquerade, and in consequence loses the man. Or
should one perhaps say 'in order' to lose the man, for the
scene, which effectively sabotages her performance of 'woman',
is repeated with different men throughout *Pilgrimage*: with
'Ted' in *Pointed Roofs*, Tremayne in *The Tunnel* and von Heber,
Hancock and Ashley-Densley in the middle and later volumes.
In each case, the same point emerges, refusing to play the part
means in effect *refusing the part*, so that for Miriam 'genuine
womanliness and the masquerade' turn out to be, in Riviere's
phrase, 'the same thing'.

Art, style and representation

> To them she was a closed book. They did not want to open it. But
> if they wanted to they could not have read it. (II, 196)

The question of 'woman' and feminine identity is, throughout
Pilgrimage, placed in relation to reading and representation. In
the first novel, for example, Miriam's attempts to copy the style
of an older woman are used to set up a series of questions
about art, style and truth, which then reverberate through the

successive chapter-novels. While imitating Fräulein Pfaff's manner 'of indulgent condescension' with students, she sees her standing,

> gracefully tall, with a curious dignified pannier-like effect about the skirt that swept from the small tightly-fitting pointed bodice, reminding her of illustrations of heroines of serials in old numbers of the Girls' Own Paper. (I, 52)

As Richardson's contemporary Oscar Wilde says, 'Life imitates art'.[9] Miriam's imitation is an imitation not of an original but a copy, not of 'truth' but of 'art' ('illustrations'). The apparently casual association at the end of the description serves to remind the reader that the transmission of 'femininity' is no simple process of copy/original, that both women are caught up in a more complex process, a chain of representations which pre-exists both of them.

This may be what Lacan calls,

> an apt moment to remind ourselves that images and symbols *for* the woman cannot be isolated from images and symbols *of* the woman.
> It is representation (*Vorstellung* in the sense in which Freud uses the term to signal something repressed), the representation of feminine sexuality, whether repressed or not, which conditions how it comes into play. . . .[10]

Miriam's conscious rejection of the masquerade is framed as a rejection of its inauthenticity, that it falsifies the 'real' woman. Her position can be read as merely the objection of a puritanical young woman to feminine affectations, an objection raised not only by New Woman heroines but in romantic fiction of the late nineteenth century generally and continuous with much earlier critiques.[11] If, however, the common element in both representation and masquerade is understood as 'something repressed', rather than something false, her predicament assumes a rather different character.

The difficulties in drawing the line between 'genuine womanliness and the masquerade' are staged in a series of scenes involving representations of women – in literature, paintings and photographs, opera and theatre. The heroine works her way through different representations of 'woman', confronting each image like someone in a hall of mirrors, searching for a reflection in which she can recognise herself.

Her failure confuses and angers her, as when she stares at a photograph of a woman in Grecian drapery entitled 'Inspiration':

> It was an Englishwoman, a large stiff square body, a coil of carefully crimped hair and a curled fringe, pretending. There were people who would say, 'What a pretty photograph', and mean it. . .the draperies and the attitude. How easy it was to take people in, just by acting. (. . .) She was not a woman, she was a *woman*. . .oh, curse it all. But men liked actresses. They liked being fooled.
>   Miriam looked closely at the photograph with hatred in her eyes. (. . .) 'You get in the way of the air, you *thing*', she muttered. (I, 399–400)

What she recognises, before she recognises it as a portrait of someone she knows (Mrs Kronen), is that the photograph is another example of the masquerade constructed for a male viewer. The representation produces a sense of suffocation because what she wants is an unmediated relation to the state of 'woman' but between her and life falls the shadow of representation (this '*thing*'). Miriam cannot articulate in speech the difference between the representation of the real ('a woman') and the representation of the idea of woman ('a *woman*'); she must use the same word. As Lacan remarks, 'images and symbols *for* the woman cannot be isolated from images and symbols *of* the woman'. The distinction can be marked typographically, but not linguistically; the italics, like the ellipses discussed earlier, supplement the words as a gesture towards the difference, the 'something repressed'.

Watching Mrs Kronen smoking a cigarette in a later scene, Miriam contrasts the image in the photograph with her own view of her, but again can only articulate that by reference to another form of representation:

> The face was uplifted as it had been in the photograph, but with all the colour, the firm bows of gold hair, the colour in the face and strong white pillar of neck, the eyes closed instead of staring upwards and the rather full mouth flattened and drooping with its weight into a sort of tragic shapeliness – like some martyr. . .that picture by Rossetti, Beata Beatrix, thought Miriam. . .perfect reality. (I, 414)

She distinguishes between representations, finding the Pre-Raphaelite painting contains more of the woman's 'reality' than the photographic portrait but the basis of the distinction, reality itself, is unrepresentable. It can only be surmised from the differences between representations.

Art and the different forms of representation are increasingly linked to her sense of male domination in the world: not only are 'all books (. . .) poisoned' but all visual representations, even new forms like those at the exhibition of Daguerre she attends in *The Tunnel*, seem to be equally determined by male attitudes. The point is dramatised in a performance of *The Merchant of Venice* where watching Portia and Nerissa on stage, the heroine decides that there was 'no reality in any of Shakespeare's women. They please men because they show women as men see them' (II, 188). This is a point she constantly returns to, insistently, dogmatically reiterates in arguments with male friends, in novel after novel. It becomes a stick she uses to beat them with, and a sticking-point which represents the impossibility of communication between the sexes:

> 'The thing most needed is for men to *recognise* their illusion. (. . .) They seem incapable of unthinking the centuries of masculine attempts to represent women only in relation to the world as known to men.'
> It was then he was angry.
> 'How else shall they be represented?'
> 'They *can't* be represented by men. Because by every word they use men and women mean different things'. (IV, 93)

Men are stuck in their systems of representation, but Miriam is also stuck – as I think the repetition of the argument in this, the ninth volume, exposes. She cannot answer the question 'How else. . .etc?', can only repeat the point (that women *can't* be represented by men) without being able to take it further – to the question, for example, of whether and how women *can* be represented by women. *Pilgrimage* portrays Miriam as stuck on the horns of a dilemma. On the one hand she recognises that there can be no access to the reality of 'woman' except through existing representations, that like her moment of recognition about religion ('the Bible is not true, it is a culture'), there may be no 'true' woman, only different cultural representations of woman which are shaped by what men want of woman. On the other hand she is haunted by a sense of what is missing from these representations, by what *she* wants, hence her growing belief that this repressed element is the 'reality' she is seeking. The gap between the desire and the representation thus comes to stand for 'the real'.

Although she reaches the despairing conclusion that all gender identity.is a mask or masquerade, she cannot relinquish her aspiration to reach beyond the mask (the symbolic) to an unmasked self, to a reality which she imagines lies behind, beyond or before representation. The pilgrimage is, in one sense, just this – the quest for 'reality'. For the protagonist, the quest for an unmasked self is linked to one of her earliest memories – the bee moment in the garden – which assumes increasing significance as her attempts to operate from the masculine position fail to bring satisfaction.

His master's voice

Under their masquerade, their masks, Miriam perceives women as being 'angry'. The term first occurs when Miriam crosses the social lines in *Honeycomb*, leaving a sofa of watching women to join the men playing billiards and smoking, 'breaking out at last a public defiance of the freemasonry of women' (I, 436). From this vantage point, she surveys the other side:

> 'Ragbags, bundles of pretence,' she thought, as she confronted the women. They glanced up with cunning eyes. They looked small and cringing. She rushed on, sweeping them aside. . . .Who had made them so small and cheated and for all their smiles so angry? What was it they wanted? What was it women wanted that always made them so angry? (I, 436)

Although her initial question starts with a point about agency, what causes 'their' condition, it is, one might say, a male question, asked from a masculine position. As the narrative emphasises, the women themselves are swept aside. Taking her father's part within the family, positioning herself within the discourse of the father(s), her questions echo those of Nietzsche and Freud's later 'Was will das Weib?'.[12] The form of the question, situating 'women/them' as objects of the enquiry, aligns her with a whole Western tradition seeking a solution to the woman question, mastery over the 'problem' of women. As such it is an unmistakable sign of her masculine identification. (Woolf, in *A Room of One's Own*, later turns the question around, demanding what made the professor, the 'subject' of the enquiry, so angry.) In the later novels of *Pilgrimage*, the sense of 'anger' attributed to women provides a link to her own state which leads into a new 'feminist' position. At this stage however, although conscious that she is acting out a male role in this scene, Miriam appears unaware that the doll-like 'bundles' are creatures of her own, male-identified fears.

What she does become aware of, increasingly, is that whether operating from either a masculine or feminine position, she is in a *false* position, because either position involves 'something repressed'. If the feminine position conceals her phallic will to power behind the veil of femininity, a masculine position is a denial of her (female) body and the feminine within. Her early positionings are an imitation of the paternal function, an impersonation of her father or father-figures. When exasperated, for example, with her employer Mrs Corrie over 'some womanish overdoing it' (. . .) She felt as if she were representing Mr Corrie' (I, 393). Later in the same novel, writing to an elderly admirer 'in a clear bold hand (. . .) like his own, but stronger', she realises that he will,

> hear a man's voice, pater's voice talking behind it and not like it. Me. He'll be a little afraid of it. She felt her hard self standing there as she wrote, and shifted her feet a little, raising one heel from the ground, trying to feminise her attitude; but her hat was hard against her forehead, her clothes would not flow. (I, 418–19).

The passage presents a woman consciously 'trying to feminise her attitude', adopting a physical posture she thinks will represent a feminine position, but despite her female body and feminine clothing, she fails, it is implied, to shift the 'attitude' within. Traces of her father's voice appear in her writing and the masculine identification, 'her hard self', remains in place. The passage can also be read as an allusion to the general problems of a woman writing: the ways in which her speech and writing must traverse the discourse of the father and the difficulties of 'feminising' writing itself.

Although traditional terms ('hard' as against 'flow') are used to represent masculinity and femininity, the effect is not to reinforce the traditional categories. In fictional representations of women in the nineteenth century, including New Woman fiction, gender identity is treated for the most part as a direct relation between body and subject unmediated by the unconscious or language,[13] whereas the technique of *Pilgrimage* in this and other scenes focuses on the effects of unconscious conflicts within language and consciousness. Gender identity is represented not as simple or fixed, a matter of biology or social conditioning, but as a complex series of provisional positions. In Richardson's short story 'Summer', for example, the heroine in the absence of father or brothers, takes up an honorary male position in relation to her old aunts and receives an acceptance and approval not given her as a woman. The story dramatises the way in which the position taken will be a relational one, related in this case to the group interaction rather than the anatomy of the subject. *Pilgrimage*, similarly, insists not only that a woman may wish to take up a masculine position, but examines the points at which that wish may be acted upon, and a cross-gender position adopted.

Outside the family group, Miriam finds the masculine position – especially in relation to men – a precarious one, dependent on the goodwill of a sponsoring male, which when withdrawn may result in humiliation. A key example of this occurs in *Honeycomb*, where she is drawn into an argument about law and the truth at a Newlands dinner party, until she disagrees with her host and is snubbed into silence.

> He dropped her and took a lead coming from a man at the other end of the table. (I, 442)

The children's governess may be humoured while smoking or playing billiards, but when she publicly challenges her male employer, a leading QC, in a discussion of the law, she must be cut down to her proper size. The contradiction between her internal position (masculine therefore equal) and her position in the external world (feminine, without the power or privileges of the male in her society) comes sharply and comically into view. In her subsequent rage and disillusion, she begins to formulate her opposition to a male rationality which seeks explanations of an event (here 'a crime') in terms of single causes, which refuses to 'take the thing back into the mists of time' (I, 442). Her own approach, she decides, is holistic: any single event must be considered as part of a network of causes and effects, no part of which can be isolated and called 'the truth'. If no single event or argument can be extrapolated from its context, the relation between Miriam's intellectual argument here and the emotional context in which it takes shape must also be taken together. Its consolatory function is placed before the reader not to explain it (away) but as a part of its meaning.

Miriam crosses class as well as gender boundaries at the bourgeois dinner party in *Honeycomb*, but her masculine pretensions fare no better in the *déclassé* world of Bohemia. Visiting Ruscino's café (the Café Royal?) with Mr Mendizabal in *Interim*, she finds it full of 'worldly, wicked, happy people' and is elated by the lack of national or class divisions:

> It was a heaven, a man's heaven, most of the women were there with men, somehow watchful and dependent, but even they were forced to be free from troublings and fussings whilst they were there...the wicked cease from troubling and the weary are at rest.... She was there as a man, a free man of the world, a continental, a cosmopolitan, a connoisseur of women. (II, 394)

Wanting her share of this heaven, her masculine identifications come to the fore to enable her to enjoy the best position 'as a man'. Since this seems to involve a specular enjoyment of women, she begins to watch the other women as a 'connoisseur' might, but her first remark betrays her inexperience:

> 'Voilà une petite qui est jolie', she remarked judicially.
> 'Une jeune fille avec ses parents', rebuked Mr Mendizabal. (II, 395)

The heroine has blundered. She attempts to place herself in the position of the male viewer as 'judge' but is not initiated in the masculine codes which distinguish between a 'fille' and a 'jeune fille avec ses parents', between an unrespectable girl and a respectable one. Her failure may be simply attributed to youth and inexperience and Mendizabal's rebuke that of a connoisseur to a novice but it effectively punctures her masculine (im)posture. His words imply a strict line between types of women, but they also imply another kind of line. A gentleman in café society, Mendizabal implies, enjoys talking only about a woman he may enjoy ('une fille'); what one may not enjoy in the flesh ('une jeune fille avec ses parents') one may not enjoy talking about.[14] Since Miriam is *all talk* in this

respect, this is a refinement she cannot appreciate, and she
finds his words 'meaningless'. In a male world she is not fitted
to be a judge any more than an advocate. She is reproved for
stepping out of line, as she is snubbed for being out of order
at the dinner party; in both cases, her transgression serves as
a comment not only upon her sexual predicament but upon
the sexual order and divisions which have brought it into
being.

Miriam, however, most frequently takes up a masculine
position in relation to women (her mother and a succession
of feminine figures) and in her relation to music. Music, as
the least representational of art forms, seems to provide a
scope which literature and the visual arts do not. The sense
of power and control generated by her skills as a pianist
become symbolic, for the character, of the masculine or 'phallic
position' – what Nietzsche would call the 'desire to be more'.
The exercise of this power, as already observed in the
Mendelssohn/Beethoven scene, involves the renunciation of
other forms of power. Another scene with the piano, at the
end of *Honeycomb*, where Miriam attempts to use her piano-
playing to distract her mother from incipient 'hysteria', stages
this in a particularly interesting way:

> Nothing could happen as long as she could keep on playing like
> that. It made the music seem like a third person in the room. It
> was a new way of playing. She would try it again when she was
> alone. It made the piece wonderful. . .traceries of tone shaping
> themselves one after another, intertwining, and stopping against
> the air. . .tendrils on a sunlit wall. . . . She had a clear conviction
> of manhood. . .that strange hard feeling that was always twining
> between her and the things people wanted her to do and to be.
> Manhood with something behind it that understood. This time it
> was welcome. It served. She asserted it, sadly feeling it mould the
> lines of her face. (I, 471)

The passage implies that, for Miriam, playing the piano, like
'playing' a masculine role, has a defensive function ('It
served'). It intervenes between the two women ('like a third person'),
between the mother's hysteria and the daughter's fear of
finding herself in the same position. It suggests the daughter's
need to mark her separation from the mother as well as her
desire to appease the mother and to relieve her suffering. As
such it is 'welcome'. But the 'conviction of manhood' also

brings with it a sense of loss ('sadly feeling'). Why? Is it because Miriam cannot be in two places at once, cannot occupy a masculine and feminine position at the same moment?

> All speaking beings must line themselves up on one side or the other of this division, but anyone can cross over and inscribe themselves on the opposite side from that to which they are anatomically destined.[15]

Looking both ways

> I am something between a man and a woman; looking both ways. (II, 187)

At different points in the narrative Miriam inscribes herself on different sides of the sexual divide, crossing from one side to the other. As in Virginia Woolf's *Orlando* 'a vacillation from one sex to the other takes place', but although Miriam may 'vacillate', she can only operate from one position at a time. Her position is usually framed as an *either/or* rather than a *both*. In *A Room of One's Own* a Utopian vision of androgyny is offered as a resolution to the problems of a (gender) divided consciousness, but in *Pilgrimage* no such solution seems possible.

Both in writing and in playing the piano, Miriam feels herself in a masculine position; they give her a 'voice' and a sense of mastery but in both cases she becomes aware that this performance involves a loss of some kind. In her account of the development of woman, Kristeva argues that:

> The daughter is handed the keys to the symbolic order when she identifies with her father: only there is she recognised not in herself but against her rival, the vaginal, *jouissante* mother. Thus at the price of censuring herself as a woman, she will be able to bring to triumph her henceforth sublimated sadistic attacks on the mother whom she has repressed and with whom she will never cease to fight, either (as a heterosexual) by identifying with her, or (as a homosexual) by pursuing her as erotic object. (1977b: 30, 1986: 150)

Reading *Pilgrimage* in these terms one might argue that Miriam in the early novel-chapters is presented as her father's daughter and that this position allows her a place and a voice within the socio-symbolic order, but at a price – 'the price of censuring herself as a woman'. However, for a number of reasons (discussed in the next chapter), this identification with the father begins to give way to the call of the mother. Again, according to Kristeva the masculine, paternal identification is only,

> a fragile envelope, incapable of staving off the irruption of this conflict, of this love which has bound the little girl to her mother, and which then, like black lava, had lain in wait for her all along the path of her desperate attempts to identify with the symbolic paternal order. (1986: 157)

In Miriam's life, this conflict and this love are continually irrupting, activated by falling in love and her attempts at art. As she struggles to understand the conflict, she considers the question of her relation to her mother and father, of whether she is the daughter of her mother or of her father:

> Within me. . .the *third* child, the longed-for son, the two natures, equally matched, mingle and fight? It is their struggle that keeps me adrift, so variously interested and strongly attracted, now here, now there? Which will win?. . . . Feeling so identified with both, she could not imagine either of them set aside. Then her life *would* be the battlefield of her two natures. (III, 250)

Although this passage refers to the hereditary aspect of the relation to her father and mother, it can equally be read as a description of psychic conflict. Miriam cannot choose between her dual inheritance (or identifications) and refusing to repress either, she resolves to live out the conflict. In Nietzschean terms, one might say that the impossibility of the dialectic locks her into a structure of opposition (a 'battlefield'), transcendence of which is either a fantasy or an acceptance of the condition as unresolvable. The text of *Pilgrimage* does not put forward 'a marriage of opposites' as either possible or desirable, it affirms the unresolvable nature of sexual difference within the symbolic. The psychic world of the heroine ('her two natures') may be bisexual[16] but she lives in a social order which rigidly defines its subjects as either masculine or feminine.

In *Clear Horizon* Miriam moves constantly between her masculine and feminine identifications, between her love for a man (Hypo) and her love for a woman (Amabel). In both cases the clue as to which of Miriam's 'two natures' comes into play, at which point, is linked to the relationship with the mother. If the question of 'woman' is inextricably tied to representation, the question of feminine sexuality appears to be inextricably tied to the maternal, to the figure of the mother.

Chapter Five

Looking back (at the mother)

It is there, in the analysis of her difficult relation to her mother
and to her own difference from everybody else, men and women,
that a woman encounters the enigma of the 'feminine'.

(Kristeva, 1977: 499)

The turn to the father. . .expresses hostility to her mother; it results
from an attempt to win her mother's love; it is a reaction to
powerlessness vis-à-vis maternal omnipotence and to primary
identification. Every step of the way, as the analysts describe it, a
girl develops her relationship to her father while looking back at
her mother – to see if her mother is envious, to make sure she is
in fact separate, to see if she can in this way win her mother, to
see if she is really independent. Her turn to her father is both an
attack on her mother and an expression of love for her.

(Chodorow, 1978: 126)

Looking back is, in more than one sense, what *Pilgrimage* is
all about. It looks back on a lifetime, to the acquisition of a
woman's femininity, to the construction of her consciousness,
to the pathways taken by the pilgrim in the course of her life's
journey. *Her* movements may be forwards, backwards, sideways
or blocked, but in the novel-sequence the movement is a
circular one, the retracing of an enormous loop of time bringing
protagonist and reader towards the point of time where the
protagonist begins writing. What Miriam begins writing at the
end of the sequence is, in other words, the novel that the
reader holds in her hand. We are reading what she began

writing as she writes 'While I write' (IV, 657). At this point, the journey comes full circle, for reader and writer.

Pilgrimage is a *Bildungsroman* which is also a *Künstlerroman* (a story of an *artist's* development). In the *Bildungsroman*, the voyage of self-discovery is teleological, it leads inexorably towards the moment from which the protagonist begins her 'looking back'.

> The unfolding of the text is directed toward the goal of retrospective self-knowledge, and all aspects of the text gain their significance in relation to the developmental plot.[1]

Despite its apparent 'plotlessness', *Pilgrimage* is organised in relation to this goal and the disparity between the perspective of the narrator and the protagonist, noticeable in the earlier chapter-novels, gradually diminishes. The two perspectives eventually converge in the present tense of 'While I write'. The increasing use of the first-person in this last novel may be read *not* simply as the result of a failure to revise, as some critics maintain,[2] but a strategy consistent with the use of the *Bildung* form – a use which looks back to the German Romantics and forward to the feminist *Bildungsromane* in the late twentieth century.[3] Richardson signals her dialogue with the Romantics in the reference to Schiller at the end of the novel-sequence and explicitly in her 1938 Preface, which quotes from Goethe's *Wilhelm Meister*. Although *Pilgrimage* is also scattered with references to Wordsworth's *Prelude*, it is, thematically and formally, much closer to *Wilhelm Meister* and the song from this novel (*'Kennst du das Land, wo die Zitronen bluhn?'*) is repeated at intervals throughout *Pilgrimage*.

In *Wilhelm Meister*, Wilhelm's problem is that he cannot make a 'connection'[4] which will bring the various incidents and parts of his life into a meaningful shape. His search for 'the whole ring of his life' is like Miriam's search for 'the hidden shape of things' (IV, 171). *Pilgrimage* ends not in marriage, the traditional metaphor for the social contract with which most *Bildungsromane* close, but, like *Wilhelm Meister*, in the solitude necessary for writing: 'Still feel sure when I am writing, a loneliness that now may encircle the rest of my life' (IV, 657). The driving force of the novel series, one might say, is to bring various parts of Miriam's life, from the earliest memory of the bee moment in the garden to the events of the adult life, into a shape or pattern. Looking back, the contemplation of the past is a quest for 'a sense of the whole'.

But unlike *Wilhelm Meister* where the subjective, spiritual pole of human development is hived off into the story of the Beautiful Soul, 'safely contained as a posthumous insert',[5] *Pilgrimage* is specifically concerned with the spiritual and psychological development of a *woman*. Wilhelm's sexual identity is never really in question, whereas Miriam's always is, and the looking back is a retracing of the stages which led towards Miriam's identity as a gendered subject.

The shadow of the mother

In her article entitled 'What are men to Dorothy Richardson?', Gloria Fromm traces the importance of Miriam's father through a series of relationships with men: Pastor Lahmann and Bob Greville, Hancock and Densley, Shatov and Wilson and others. Both major and minor characters, Fromm argues, owe much of their significance to Miriam's relationship with her father.

> Although Mr Henderson scarcely appears in the novel, he casts his long shadow across *Pilgrimage* to point up the patterns formed by Miriam's other relationships. Without him the content of the ongoing narrative involving middle-aged men would not be manifest, nor would the picaresque tale of her relations with a series of young men.[6]

One could argue a symmetrical case: that Mrs Henderson who also 'scarcely appears' in the novel, also casts a long shadow pointing up the patterns formed by Miriam's other relationships. It would indeed be possible to relate these patterns – particularly with the women characters – directly back to the mother, rather than the father, and thus to claim *Pilgrimage* as a mother–daughter novel. But the attempt here is to argue that *both* these figures are manifest in Miriam's other relationships. Her relations with male and female figures in the text are governed by her transference relations with the mother, but that mother is always defined in relation to the father, his presence or his absence. In other words, the mother/daughter relation in the text cannot be understood without the father because the mother–daughter dyad is always *triangulated* by the father. One does not move without the other, but they do not move together, one might say.

Just as there is more than one 'I' in Miriam, so there is more than one 'mother' in *Pilgrimage*. In the first three chapter-novels, there are references to the 'Mrs Henderson' whose presence comforts the daughter during the onset of menstruation, who escorts Miriam to her teaching interview, who tells her her nainsook blouse is still wearable. This 'social' mother is barely characterised as an individual, although her unequal position within the marriage, presented in several key scenes, is prominent in her daughter's consciousness. After Miriam's return from Hanover, anxieties about the father's financial position are gradually overshadowed by anxieties over the mother's nervous 'illness', which culminates in her suicide during a visit to Brighton with her daughter. 'Mrs Henderson' comes to a violent end at the end of the third novel, just as her third daughter begins to identify with her as a woman, to realise that: 'There was something she had always wanted for herself. . .even mother' (I, 472).

Alongside this Mrs Henderson, the external mother, other voices appear in the text, voices of a maternal imago who lives on in Miriam's unconscious long after the death of the 'real' mother – and after the sign for Teetgens Teas, which represents that death, has lost its effect.[7] These voices project what one might call Miriam's 'oedipal' and 'pre-oedipal' mother figures and it is these internal objects which haunt the daughter, accompanying her to the very last pages of the novel. The mother who tells Miriam 'You ought to have been a man, Mimmy' (I, 193), seems to represent the oedipal mother, an image of womanliness against which the rivalrous daughter feels powerless, inadequate, 'unfeminine'. It is this aspect of her mother, or this relation to the mother, which is presented in the form of a dream at the start of the novel. The night before her departure for Germany, she dreams she is standing in a room in the German school, being looked at by the women staff:

> They had dreadful eyes – eyes like the eyes of hostesses she remembered, eyes she had seen in trains and buses, eyes from the old school. They came and saw her as she was, without courage,

without funds or good clothes or beauty, without charm or interest, without even the skill to play a part. They looked at her with loathing. (I, 21)

Like all the dreams narrated in *Pilgrimage* this one is presented without analysis. There is no subject who is presumed to know, the reader is left to interpret the significance of the dream material within the narrative. Here, one might say, the dream serves as a reminder that though departing for 'das deutsche Vaterland. . .all woods and mountains and tenderness' (I, 21), the protagonist cannot leave her internal world, which contains this 'mother', behind her. She takes the 'dreadful eyes', with her to the 'Fatherland' where indeed she 'finds' them once more in Fräulein Pfaff. Those who do not know their own history, the narrator implies, are doomed to repeat it.

She also takes with her traces of another maternal figure, which she hears in the voice which comforts her at her moment of crisis with Fräulein Pfaff (I, 169), which she finds again in Mrs Corrie's 'absolute confidence and admiration. . .like mother' (I, 359) and which she hears occasionally in the voices of her sisters or other women:

> The low, secure, untroubled tone of a woman's voice. There was nothing like it on earth. . . If you had once heard it. . .in your own voice, and the voice of another woman responding. . .everything was there. (I, 464)

'There was nothing like it on earth. . .everything was there.' The passage conjures up a state of bliss, a mixing of memory with desire. Her memory of a woman's voice contains the desire for a perfect relationship free from either conflict or contradiction where one might be held 'secure, untroubled'. It is a fantasy state ('nothing like it on earth'), from which nothing has been lost ('everything was there'). The passage is remarkably close to Cixous' image of the maternal poetic voice, which links it back to the breast and the original mother–child relation:

> Voice. Inexhaustible milk is rediscovered. The lost mother. Eternity: voice mixed with milk. (1986: 173)

The passage thus represents Miriam's desire to return not to the social mother, 'Mrs Henderson' before her illness, nor to the rivalrous mother of the oedipal phase, but to a fantasy of the pre-oedipal mother – *before* the turn to the father. Once again this maternal imago is defined in relation to the father (his absence), if only because it constitutes a denial of the father as third term. In the fantasy, nothing comes between 'your own voice and the voice of another woman responding'.

The turn to the father

The process by which the girl child turns from her first love-object (the mother or mother-figure) to the father (or his representative) is the subject of very different theorisations by psychoanalysts and feminist theorists.[8] The process is crucial in order to explain both how the female child's passage through the oedipal phase differs from that of the male, and how her entry into the symbolic order (language, sexual difference, culture) will define her 'feminine' position. Here I want to read the ways in which Miriam Henderson's position is presented in the text in the light of Kristeva's theories of psychosexual development, but with reference to a number of other (different) arguments.

According to Freud, the girl child is driven out of the attachment to the mother through envy of the penis and she 'enters the Oedipus situation as though into a haven'.[9] For Kristeva too, although the mechanism is differently explained, the female child must relinquish the pre-oedipal attachment to the mother (the 'semiotic' space) in order to gain a place within the symbolic and avoid psychosis. In Western monotheistic societies she faces a stark choice: either mother-identification or father-identification. If she identifies with the mother, the maternal space, she has access to 'vaginal *jouissance*' but forfeits a place in time and history. If, on the other hand, she identifies herself with the father, denying the mother, she is none the less biologically female and the father-identification remains precarious. The reactivation of the semiotic, the call of the mother, puts her position within the symbolic at risk – 'makes her ecstatic, nostalgic, or mad' (1977b: 30).

Pilgrimage offers its own reading of precisely this dilemma, these processes as they are repeated and re-enacted by Miriam

Henderson. Her ambivalent relation to her original love-objects is manifested in her relations with women and men in turn. 'Feeling so identified with both, she could not imagine either of them set aside' (III, 250). For her, there seems to be no 'haven', no route to 'normal femininity';[10] she can come to rest in neither the pre-oedipal (semiotic) nor the oedipal (symbolic). The novel-sequence is situated, one might say, in the interplay between the symbolic and the semiotic, constantly turning from one to the other.

In the early chapter-novels, Miriam's masculine identifications, or what Freud would call her 'masculinity complex' is presented in relation to the fact that she is *assigned* a gendered identity partly by force of parental expectation. She is positioned as the 'longed for son' somewhat in the way that Stephen Gordon is presented in *The Well of Loneliness*.[11] As the sequence develops, however, this determinist explanation comes under increasing pressure and several alternatives are introduced. In particular, this version of events does not explain the subject's participation in the parental fantasy: why does Miriam refuse the feminine position, what is in it for her, what desires of the girl child would this assigned masculine subject-position meet and fulfil?

These questions are articulated with more and more urgency in the middle and later volumes as Miriam cannons continually between different subject positions: 'I am like a man' or 'I wouldn't have a man's *consciousness* – for anything' (II, 149). Parental desires, heredity, socialisation are all canvassed as possible explanations for Miriam's confused sexual position. The reader follows Miriam (analysand) and her narrator's (analyst) progress through a maze of information and analysis. One may ask how else an ambitious and intellectual girl in the late nineteenth century could express herself except by the assumption of masculinity, but this kind of cultural interpretation, while it is allowed a certain explanatory power is not, however, the only one circulating in the text.

It is possible, for example, to read Miriam's sexual ambi-valence in terms of the Kristevan theory, as an oscillation between power and denial, but it can also be read in terms of the 'masquerade' outlined earlier. If the feminine masquerade can be understood as an attempt to please and pacify the father (and other males), the 'masculinity complex' can be seen as an attempt to appease the mother, to reassure her (and her substitutes) that the daughter does not wish to usurp or harm her. (In Freudian theory it would also constitute a denial of 'castration'.) In Miriam's case, there is some textual evidence that mother and daughter have together taken refuge in the assumed 'masculinity' of the daughter, and that this pattern was established from an early period – hence 'You ought to have been a man, Mimmy.' The masculine position releases her from unconscious rivalry and guilt and both mother and daughter are protected by Miriam's repudiation of femininity – the notion of her 'difference'.[12]

Several things bring this early positioning into crisis: the testing of the masculine position outside the family circle; the new identification with the mother which develops during her breakdown; and the daughter's guilt and grief at the death of the mother. These events produce a new scenario in which certain elements are brought to consciousness. Unlike her father, the men she encounters outside the family treat her not as an honorary male but as a 'woman', treat her in fact as her father often treats her mother, with gallantry and contempt. Being positioned by these males as 'woman' in a world in which gender roles are sharply polarised, enables the protagonist to look again at her relation to father and mother. Returning home for her sisters' marriages, she hears the voices of her father and mother in the next room arguing:

A voice level and reassuring; going up now and again into a hateful amused falsetto. Miriam refused to listen. She had never been so near before. Of course they had talked all their lives; an endless conversation; he laying down the law. . .no end to it. . .the movement of his beard as he spoke, the red lips shining through the fair moustache. . .(. . .) he had a ruddy skin. . .healthy.

A tearful, uncertain voice. . .

'Don't, mother. . .don't, don't. . .he can't understand. . .Come to me! Come in here. . . Well, well!'. . . A loud clear tone moving near the door, 'Leave it all to nature, my dear. . .'

They're talking about Sally and Harriett. . . He is *amused*. . .like when he says 'the marriage service begins with "dearly beloved" and ends with "amazement". . .'

She turned about, straining away from the wall and burying her head in her pillow. (I, 460)

As the unseen listener realises, the argument is about the daughters' sexual education and the father's anticipation of their sexual initiation – he is acting out the female role in a 'hateful amused falsetto'. The scene is part of a complex meditation on bourgeois marriage relations staged in this chapter of *Honeycomb*, but it is also a critical scene in terms of Miriam's development. It dramatises with great force and economy a complex shift in Miriam's relation to each parent (how having at first 'refused to listen'. . . 'She turned about. . .'). Having personal experience of the male 'laying down the law', with Mr Corrie in the previous chapter, she is now in a position to hear its effect on her mother and to identify with her mother's reaction. The 'precarious' identification with the father seems to break down at this point.

In this scene her mother's condition does not inspire impatience but a new terror and pity, after which she vows to renounce all love for the father. The resolution extends beyond her father into nearly all her subsequent relationships with men; the unconscious guilt and reparation to the mother is an active element in her sabotage of various male relationships and plays a part in the renunciation of Michael Shatov in *Deadlock* and of Hypo Wilson in *Clear Horizon*:

> Something seemed to shriek within her, throwing him off, destroying, flinging him away. Never again anything but contempt. . .
> She lay weak and shivering in the uncomfortable little bed. Her heart was thudding in her throat and in her hands. . . beloved. . .beloved. . .a voice, singing:
>
> > So, ear-ly *in* the mor-ning,
> > My beloved – my beloved.
>
> Silence, darkness and silence. (I, 460)

The experience is traumatic because it brings her parents' sexual relation nearer than ever before, it forces her to see them in a new light and for the first time to take the mother's part against the father 'he can't understand. . . . Come to me! Come in here. . . .' The disillusionment with the father produces a turning back to the mother but the new alignment is ambivalent and ambiguously presented. The position of the words 'beloved' between ellipses leaves it uncertain *who* is

'my beloved' in this instance – the father she is renouncing
or the mother she wants to win back.

On the night before her mother's suicide, Miriam has another
dream. Like the earlier one, the dream is narrated without
commentary. The two scenes of the dream and Miriam's
awakening are presented in a single paragraph, set off from
the rest of the text by its spacing. In the first scene of the
dream, Miriam watches someone playing the piano, the two
(player and listener) are apparently alone in a small music
room. The face of the pianist in the dream is that of an old
schoolfriend, Lilla, which she sees as 'stern and manly'. . .'manly and unconscious' above the hands playing 'steadily and vigorously':

> Miriam listened incredulous at the certainty with which she played
> out her sadness and her belief. It shocked her that Lilla should
> know so deeply and express her lonely knowledge so ardently.
> (. . .) She and Lilla were one person, the same person. Deep down
> in every one was sorrow and certainty. A faint resentment filled
> her. She turned away. . . (I, 484)

'Lilla' in the dream is a figure in whom Miriam recognises
herself ('one person, the same person'), but the recognition
brings 'a faint resentment' and she turns away. In Freudian
theory, this composite figure is the 'phallic mother' ('manly'),
whose lack of phallus once recognised ('sorrow and certainty'),
causes the daughter to turn away in resentment[13] but it can also
be read as the subject's wish to return to the undifferentiated
mother–child bond ('one person, the same person'), as a visit
to Kristeva's 'semiotic' succeeded by a turning back to the
symbolic.

In the second part of the dream, the scene slides into a large
music room, full of seated forms:

> Lilla was at the piano, her foot on the low pedal, her hands raised
> for a crashing chord. They came down, collapsing faintly on a blur
> of wrong notes. Miriam rejoiced in her heart. What a fiend
> I am. . .what a fiend, she murmured, her heart hammering
> condemnation. Someone was sighing harshly; to be heard; in the
> darkness; not far off; fully conscious she glanced at the blind.
> (I, 485).

This dream scene clearly stages Miriam's rivalry with Lilla and
her guilt about that rivalry. But the contiguity of the dream

and the awakening in the paragraph also makes the connection between the mother and Lilla, the displacement of emotion from a major to a minor figure. Awakening from the dream, the daughter becomes conscious of her mother ('Someone was sighing harshly; to be heard'). If one takes 'Lilla' as a screen figure or 'blind' for the mother, the two parts of the dream signify the two stages of the daughter's relation to the mother: her initial shock and resentment at the newly discovered 'sorrow' of the mother which causes her to turn away; and the rivalrous and guilty feelings towards the oedipal mother which succeed that turn. Placed at the end of the third novel, the dream can thus be read as a condensation of the psychic development of the heroine. Miriam's guilt about the mother is textually established *before* the suicide of Mrs Henderson is narrated. Her later feelings of guilt 'she was a murderess. This was the hidden truth of her life' (III, 75) will then refer not merely to the fact that her mother died while in her care, but to the rivalrous *wish* that her mother might die.

In this reading of *Pilgrimage*, the death of the mother occurs at a point of increasing identification and also increasing awareness of rivalry. Miriam enters into what Klein in 'Mourning and manic-depressive states' calls 'the depressive position'.[14] Her death locks the daughter more deeply into the defensive position adopted earlier – the 'masculinity complex' or the denial of the feminine within. If she is 'masculine' like the father, she can deny rivalry and protect the mother; she may even become what her mother desires (and lacks), and this would satisfy the infantile wish to be all that her mother desires: 'She laughed towards her mother and smiled at her until she made her blush. Ah, she thought proudly, it's I who am your husband' (I, 456).

Yet Miriam's sense of responsibility for the mother's death has other contradictory effects. If she is like her father, she is like the man who helped to drive her mother to suicide – or at least like her father's masculine-identified daughter who failed to protect her. So this too must be denied. The masculine within must be repudiated *because it is as dangerous to the mother as the feminine position of rivalry*. Having *introjected* the masculine to defend the mother, Miriam must now for the same reason *project* the 'masculine within' outwards and away from herself. At one later point Miriam even denies she is her father's daughter, claiming that 'If anything I am my mother's son' (III, 220). Dominated by these internal conflicts, she is, as she begins to realise, on the horns of a dilemma – 'something between a man and a woman, looking both ways' (II, 187), and this emerges in her relations with both men and women.

The case of Michael Shatov

After the death of the mother, Miriam enters a new stage. *The Tunnel* and *Interim* chart the development of a feminist critique of the patriarchal world she inhabits. Discovering the extent of male prejudice, feminism provides her with a political critique which corresponds to the unconscious need to repudiate the identification with the father. Although she wants the freedom to live like a man (II, 230), the protagonist struggles increasingly to dissociate herself from the masculine mind and attitudes: 'I wouldn't be a man for anything. I wouldn't have man's – *consciousness*, for anything' (II, 149). The 'masculine within' is split off and projected on to a series of men encountered, and these are energetically denounced. Some, but by no means all, of the hostility and rivalry previously directed at women is redirected towards these male figures.

In the next novel *Deadlock*, the repudiation of men is tried and tested when the protagonist meets and falls in love with a man called Michael Shatov. Despite their mutual love, she rejects his proposal of marriage and at the end of the novel-chapter renounces the relationship. Several reasons are offered for the renunciation, each with its own validity, but the number of different explanations in the narrative – almost any one of which would have been sufficient – is striking. Why this heaping up of reasons? It could be argued that the superfluity of explanations marks Miriam's difficulty in rejecting her suitor, but that would in turn raise another question, why reject what is so much desired? In terms of *this* question, and the parental 'shadows', the relationship with Shatov is one of the most crucial in *Pilgrimage*.[15]

Although Michael Shatov's proposal is rejected in *Deadlock*, their relation is not in fact terminated. 'Michael' makes a

second proposal later in the sequence, when Miriam discovers
she is pregnant with Hypo's child. He is again rejected and
this time 'handed over' to Amabel whom he marries. The
meaning of her love for Shatov and her renunciation and 'gift'
of him to another woman, is the subject of continued analysis
and revision in the later novel-chapters, _Clear Horizon_ and
March Moonlight.

From the first, the human and intellectual qualities of
the Russian student are emphasised: polyglot, widely read,
sympathetic, he challenges her dogmatic, snobbish views in a
non-authoritarian, non-adversarial way. European, intellectual,
he represents a type of masculinity she has not before
encountered in the professional, middle-class English males
she meets in the Orly household. With him she can discuss
the questions of religion and philosophy which she has pored
over in the solitude of her room, openly, and on terms of
equality: 'He forced her to think' (III, 63). Encouraged by him,
she begins her first writing – of translations. Their friendship
develops rapidly in the first few months. He is a 'father' who
shares his intellectual riches, and a 'mother' who urges her to
eat, loves her without conditions or rivalry. The growth of
Miriam's love is registered in a renewed sense of self and
surroundings; London and 'the bliss of post offices and railway
stations' (III, 86) becomes a heaven. Their first kiss is described
as a religious transfiguration, in a highly-wrought passage
where the erotic figures only as rhythm and syntactical flow:
'A voyage, swift and transforming, a sense of passing in the
midst of this marvel of flame-lit darkness' (III, 192).

The obstacles to the love-affair appear shortly after this: his
revelation that he is a Jew; his confession of previous sexual
experience with a prostitute; and her view of the impossibility
of equality in marriage and her dread of the role of 'wife' in
marriage. All these factors are given due weight in Miriam's
consciousness, and the interrelation of the issues (in the
heroine's mind) is presented with great subtlety and complexity
in the text. What is also revealed in the text, however, is that
Shatov offers to give up his religion and that Miriam 'forgives'
his experience with the prostitute. These are not it seems the
just impediments to the marriage. Miriam's confusion about
her motives is emphasised:

> Long grappling in darkness against the inexorable images, she fell
> back at last upon wordless repudiation, and again the gulf of
> isolation opened before her. (. . .) The smallest glance in the
> direction of even the simulation of acceptance brought a panic
> sense of treachery. . . . (III, 209)

Who or what this would be treachery to is left open.

In the next novel, *Revolving Lights*, Miriam states that she
had felt her 'male relatives would have the right to *beat* [her]'
had she married her Jewish lover (III, 260) thus giving a racial
meaning to her sense of treachery. But this statement is a
simplification of the initial reaction, given as follows:

> Many people would think, as she had in the beginning, that he was
> an intellectual Frenchman, different from the usual 'Frenchman'; a
> big-minded cosmopolitan at any rate; a proud possession. The
> mysterious fact of Jewishness could remain in the background. . .the
> hidden flaw. . .as there was always a hidden flaw in all her
> possessions. (III, 193)

The 'fact of Jewishness' is here named as a 'flaw' which might
seem to explain the rejection of the beloved and thus resolve
the issue. But even given the general anti-Semitism of the
period[16] and the particular xenophobia of the character, the
statement is a peculiar one. Why is the man's Jewish identity
linked to this Christian girl's sense of her past? As the tell-
tale ellipses once again signal, there is some element missing.
Miriam's thought links this 'flaw' to 'the hidden flaw in all
her possessions', but the nature of the link, and of the earlier
flaws, is left for the reader to construe.

Is the link to the father and male sexuality? Is Shatov's 'flaw'
like the one Miriam discovered in her father – the one that
caused her to renounce *him*? Shatov's use of a prostitute could
certainly be said to exhibit the same attitude to women shown
by Mr Henderson and shared by 'the whole male mind of
Europe' (II, 208). In which case 'acceptance' of Shatov might
indeed seem a 'treachery' to her dead mother, and the
renunciation of Michael would then seem to repeat the earlier
renunciation of the father. Or is the link not to the father but
to the mother, whose 'flaw' (the mysterious 'fact of castration')
had at an earlier point caused Miriam to turn away from her?
According to Otto Weininger, whose ideas preoccupy Miriam
at this point, Jews are like women, 'lacking in personality' and

individuality;[17] in which case Miriam's recoil from Michael could be read as the repetition of her earlier repudiation of femininity as 'flawed' or incomplete. Just as one train of thought conceals another, one over-determined set of reasons for the renunciation seems to cover another, and the relationship reaches the standstill implied in the title. A 'deadlock' is 'the case when matters have become so complicated that all is at a complete standstill' (Chambers Dictionary).

Paradoxically, this deadlock leads to a new realisation: that the 'flaw' is not just in Shatov but in any object she may take as her desire ('all my possessions'), since any love-object, male or female, will be lacking or 'flawed'. Only God, the image of perfect love, is not. The point prepares the ground for the next stage of Miriam's spiritual and emotional journey: not only are all human love-objects 'flawed', desire is necessarily unattainable. 'The Catholics know that desire can never be satisfied. You must not desire God. You must love. I can't do that' (III, 283). 'Love' becomes an intransitive verb and God, the image of 'perfect love' signifies both the human desire for love and its impossibility. In order to reach *this* aporia, however, she has first to make a different trial of love: with a woman whose name signifies love and beauty.

The case of Amabel

The introduction of Amabel in the tenth novel of *Pilgrimage* marks a new stage in the pilgrim's sexual progress. *Dawn's Left Hand* is an account of two interlinking stories: Miriam's love for the younger woman, and her sexual relationship with an older married man, the husband of an old friend. In both relationships, Miriam takes up a feminine position, a maternal role as a 'Flemish madonna' (IV, 231). With other women friends, Eleanor Dear, Selina Holland and later 'Jean', she assumes a masculine position, 'lover-like' as she says (II, 439), but with Amabel she is 'the beloved'. As the initial chapters establish, the new positionality is produced not merely by Amabel, but by a shift in the protagonist's inner world.

Miriam returns from Oberland with a 'strange new light within her' (IV, 153), a light which seems to signal the end of one period and the beginning of a new. She returns to some major changes – the break with Selina, Hypo's declaration of love and Densley's proposal – but these external events seem secondary to the internal changes. These are registered, once again, through her reaction to the advertising sign for Teetgens Teas:

> the grimed gilt lettering that *forced me to gaze into the darkest moment of my life and to remember that I had forfeited my share in humanity for ever and must go quietly and alone until the end.*
>
> *And now their power has gone. They can bring back only the memory of a darkness and horror, to which, then, something has happened, begun to happen?* (IV, 155–6) (Italics in text)

Something has begun to happen to the guilt and anxiety following her mother's suicide. The period of mourning characterised by obsessive attempts at reparation and withdrawal from relationships seems to have ended[18] and the stage seems set for a new engagement. As this passage exemplifies, something also happens to the style in this novel: an increasing use of flashback, of italics and passages of self-analysis in the first-person mode. Through the alternation of third- and first-person narration, Miriam is alternately positioned as object then subject of the narration, in a shot-reverse-shot movement which underlines the question of positionality in Miriam's new relationships.

From their first meeting the two women are strongly attracted and despite 'the warning voice within' (IV, 175), Miriam feels 'embarked in sunlight upon an unknown quest' (IV, 188). Amabel in public performs the feminine masquerade, graceful, elegant, full of 'plastic poses' (IV, 191), and privately asserts to Miriam her conviction that men and women can never directly communicate. She regards Miriam not with the 'dreadful eyes' of other women but uncritically, adoringly, positioning her as a *mater dolorosa*, 'set and kept upon a pinnacle and worshipped for wisdom and purity' (IV, 191). This projection, as Miriam realises, calls into being some faculty or desire within her, Miriam:

> For if indeed, . . .this emerging quality were the very root of her being, then she was committed for life to the role allotted to her by the kneeling girl. (IV, 192)

Amabel's declaration of love – 'I love you' written in soap on

her mirror – finds a response in Miriam and she re-enters a
world of shared intimacy in which for a time nothing is
allowed to come between her own voice 'and the voice of
another woman responding'. Life with Amabel brings the
conviction that,

> nothing could compare with what Amabel had brought. Nothing
> could be better. No sharing, not even the shared being of a man
> and a woman which she sometimes envied and sometimes
> deplored, could be deeper or more wonderful than this being
> together. . . . (IV, 242)

Amabel's love in effect authorises the much postponed sexual
consummation with Hypo, an experience to which Miriam
brings a maternal rather than a sexual passion, claiming her
new lover as 'My little babe, just born' (IV, 232).

The morning after her sexual experience, Miriam sees in her
mirror three birds flying 'in the form of an elongated triangle'
(IV, 259), a visual experience which is described as leaving her
'thrilled from head to foot with the sense of having shared
their swift and silent flight' (IV, 259). The image, one of a
series of mirror images, acts as a commentary on the previous
night's activity. What she has shared, of course, is on one level
simply the 'flight' of sexual experience. But by accepting the
role of lover, she has established her claim to a share in human
sexuality and reclaimed 'her share of humanity' which was
forfeited by her mother's death. 'Disadvantage had fallen from
her and burden, leaving a calm and delightful sense of power'
(IV, 267). By the sexual act, she enters into a triangle composed
of Hypo, Alma and herself, but that triangle like that of the
birds, takes its meaning in the text from an earlier 'elongated
triangle'. Whether or not this is an oedipal triangle, it is not
a position that she can bear to occupy for long and *Dawn's
Left Hand* ends with her return to her beloved territory of
London and Amabel.

In the next chapter-novel *Clear Horizon*, Miriam enters on a
new round of renunciations. She ends the sexual relationship
with Hypo, and believing she is now pregnant, conceives a
plan to bring Amabel and Michael Shatov together. Once
again, as with the earlier rejection of Michael Shatov, the
meaning of this disposal of Amabel is subject to considerable
analysis and revision:

Isolated with possible motives, she found herself in a maze whose partitions were mirrors.

Yet *even if it were true* that her real desire was to perform in person the social miracle of introducing one life to another, without consideration of the inclinations of either person concerned, *even if it were true* that she desired only to show off Michael and to show off Amabel, again without consideration, *even if it were true* that there was not the remotest chance of help coming from Amabel to Michael and that therefore it was she herself and not Michael, who was the pathetic fragment, so cut off and resourceless as to delight in the mere reproduction of social rituals and the illusory sense of power and of importance to be gained therefrom, it was now impossible to imagine the occasion as not taking place. *Something far away below any single, particular motive she could search out,* had made the decision, was refusing to attend to this conscious conflict and was already regarding the event as current, *even as past and accomplished.* This complete, independent response, whose motives were either undiscoverable or non-existent, might be good or bad, but was irrecoverable. (IV, 285–6) (My italics)

The compulsive repetition of 'even if it were true' drives through the convoluted syntax of the passage; it registers the unconscious within the conscious deliberations. The childish match-making is a way of disposing of Amabel and Michael, of clearing the horizon and in this sense is a repetition of earlier renunciations. Having found a blissful place in which nothing comes between her and the other woman's voice, Miriam finds it claustrophobic and turns away. Her decision, as the narrator emphasises, appears predetermined 'even as past and accomplished'.

In the account in *Clear Horizon*, Miriam appears to initiate the break: to escape from their love, 'to make sure she is in fact separate, . . . to see if she is really independent', in Chodorow's terms. In a later passage in *March Moonlight*, however, Miriam recalls the situation rather differently. Contrasting a new relationship to that with Amabel, she remembers an incident omitted from the earlier version of events:

Again and again I recalled my helpless woe when Amabel first hinted her desire for fresh people, her need to pass on, opening a gulf across which I still look back. Still, I can feel the sudden hard indifference of the wall behind us as we sat side by side across my narrow bed and still, my own surprise at the swift tears flowing quietly, resignedly, as though for long they had been prepared without my knowledge, for this inevitable moment, and

seeming, so swiftly in that instant of silent realization had I moved
back into loneliness, the witnessed grief of another. And to this
day I do not know whether she desired only to test her power, or
whether her response to my tears, her undertaking never to leave
me, was native generosity, or just a way of comforting a child.
(IV, 566–7)

In this revised account, it appears that it was Amabel who
first turned away from Miriam, and that Miriam's disposal of
Amabel was a reaction to an earlier rejection, repressed from
the earlier account. The power of the scene, the brilliantly
realised details of the hard wall, the narrow bed, etc., conveys
the emotional importance of the memory. The analepsis throws
a new light on the earlier scene in which the two women
discussed marriage to Michael Shatov. Each seems to have
been 'test(ing) her power', testing the other's love by offering
to release her to marry Shatov. Thus Miriam's gift of Michael
– 'Then marry him yourself my dear' (IV, 293) appears as a
retaliation to Amabel's earlier 'You MUST marry him!' (IV,
291). As Miriam recognises, the motives seem so complex as
to be 'undiscoverable', yet if each woman was testing the
other, then each seems to have failed the other, forcing her to
re-enact the turn away from the mother.[19] For Miriam, Amabel
seems to represent the mother who turns away, leaving her
only the turn towards the father – a case of *'Si tu détournes de
moi ton visage. . .je me tourne vers le père'.*[20]
   In the last paragraph of *March Moonlight*, Miriam is still
circling around the meaning of her relationship with Amabel,
considering the 'original' love between them and the subsequent emergence of rivalry:

> Yet all such moments, since she knew how thankfully I had given
> Michael into her hands, surprise me with their continuous
> suggestion of successful rivalry; while still the essence of our
> relationship remains untouched. Still we remain what we were to
> each other when we first met. (IV, 658)

Looking back on 'the inexpressible quality' (IV, 658) of her
relationship with Amabel in this the last paragraph of the
novel, it seems that little has been resolved. Miriam may here
assert the original dyad, ('Still we remain what we were'),
against the evidence of oedipal rivalries, but 'the form of an
elongated triangle' still sets its seal on their relationship.

Although she had given Michael 'thankfully' into Amabel's hands, and although she has given up her role of 'Dick' to Jean, no amount of hostages can release her from the rival claims of the semiotic and the symbolic – or what she earlier called her 'battlefield'.

Freud claimed in his paper 'Femininity' that there were three paths of development for the woman: neurosis, masculinity complex and normal femininity.[21] Even as she holds Michael and Amabel's child in her arms, Miriam is in effect looking back at the mother, she has still not found the pathway to the 'normal femininity' that Freud claimed existed for women. But if, in Derrida's terms, the search for 'woman' is an impossible one, Freud's construct of 'normal femininity' may be equally impossible. 'Normal femininity' could be defined as the struggle with this impossibility and *Pilgrimage*, among its other achievements, presents this struggle in a way rarely achieved before or since.

Chapter Six

The subject of writing: écriture féminine

> One must listen to her differently in order to hear an *'other meaning'*
> *which is constantly in the process of weaving itself, at the same time*
> *ceaselessly embracing words and yet casting them off to avoid becoming*
> *fixed, immobilised.*
>
> (Irigaray, 1985b: 103)

Interweaving and intersecting with the story of Miriam Henderson in *Pilgrimage* is the story of another woman called Eleanor Dear. She first appears from a home for 'decayed gentlewomen' in *The Tunnel* (II, 242), and then at intervals in the succeeding volumes, until her death from tuberculosis in *Dawn's Left Hand* (IV, 151). A young nurse existing on the borderland of genteel poverty, her difficulties with health and money underline the economic insecurity of Miriam's position; a conventional woman living in a world of feminine contrivances, she initiates Miriam into a new appreciation of the feminine which allows her access to the lost world of the mother. In the text she is significant in class, gender and psychoanalytic terms, and for Miriam 'She was central. All heaven and earth about her as she spoke' (III, 260).

Her story is given yet another meaning when, after the birth of an illegitimate child at the Bible Women's Hostel, she becomes 'a young married woman in a pretty villa, near the church' (III, 285). In nineteenth-century fictional terms, Eleanor's story is of a 'fallen woman' rescued into the respectability of marriage – 'But only because Rodkin was a child-worshipper' (III, 285). In the early twentieth century, Miriam decides, there are still only two ways of telling her story: 'To Michael, a poor pitiful thing; Rodkin's victim' (III, 284), to others an 'adventuress' (III, 284). It is while meditating on the story of Eleanor that Miriam the incipient writer articulates her objections to story-telling conventions and formulates her own narrative method:

> It is tempting to tell the story. A perfect recognizable story of a scheming unscrupulous woman; making one feel virtuous and superior; but only if one simply outlined the facts, leaving out all the inside things. Knowing a story like that from the inside, knowing Eleanor, changed all 'scandalous' stories. They were scandalous only when told? Never when thought of by individuals alone? Speech is technical. Every word. In telling things technical terms must be used; which never quite apply. To call Eleanor an adventuress does not describe her. You can only describe her by the original contents of her mind. Her own images; what she sees and thinks. (III, 285)

The problems of 'naming' Eleanor and her story are explicitly posed here. In one version, a 'victim' (too passive) in another an 'adventuress' (too active), both are male ways of naming the woman and neither describes her, because as Miriam puts it, both 'leave out all the inside things'. Each term constructs her as the object of a masculine discourse, neither presents her as subject – only 'her own images; what she sees and thinks' will do that. Eleanor's story takes up the issues raised earlier in the sequence, of the extent to which the recognition of 'reality' is governed by narrative conventions.[1] The general points about narrativity are here focused around the question of gender. Miss Dear, like Virginia Woolf's Mrs Brown in 'Mr Bennett and Mrs Brown', exemplifies the problems for a woman writing about women and the alternative method Miriam describes here is the method of *Pilgrimage*.

Richardson's rejection of linear story-based narratives and her dissatisfaction with current forms is of course common to the period. But her narrative innovations, like Woolf's, are not modernist-for-modernism's sake, but gender-motivated attempts to find alternatives to a masculinist discourse.[2] As she stated of her own method in 'Data for a Spanish publisher':

> The material that moved me to write would not fit the framework
> of any novel I had experienced. I believed myself to be, even when
> most enchanted, intolerant of the romantic and realist novel alike.
> Each, so it seemed to me, left out certain essentials. . . . (1989: 139)

The same point, the same phrase is used by Miriam within
the novel, when discussing contemporary novelists:

> The torment of all novels is what is left out. . . Bang, bang, bang,
> on they go, these men's books, like an L.C.C. tram, yet unable to
> make you forget them, the authors, for a moment. (IV, 239)

The anxiety about what is 'left out' of male fiction may be
one reason for the inclusion of enormous amounts of interior
monologue and description, for the repetition of narrative
movements which might have been condensed or composited.
The 'excessive' length is thus a symptom of the search for a
new feminine form and is crucial to Richardson's poetics of
the novel. Within the text, this search is motivated by the
heroine's growing sense that narrative conventions are simply
an organisation of the fantasies of the dominant culture and
are dependent, as Richardson wrote elsewhere, 'on a whole
set of questionable agreements and assumptions between
reader and writer'.[3] Where Joyce uses these dominant fantasies,
playfully, parodically, Richardson attempts to evade them, to
write round them, continually dispersing any 'story interest'
into Miriam's 'own images; what she sees and thinks'. In the
terms of Woolf's 'Modern fiction' essay there is 'no plot, no
comedy, no tragedy, no love interest or catastrophe in the
accepted style'.

Given the fact, as Rachel Blau DuPlessis argues in *Writing
Beyond the Ending*, 'that "story" for women typically meant
plots of seduction, courtship, the energies of quest deflected
into sexual downfall [or] the choice of a marriage partner'
(1985: 151), the refusal of story or plot in the fiction of
Richardson and Woolf may be seen as a defensive structure,
a form of resistance which itself testifies to the power of the
dominant narrative forms.

In a similar way, the deferral of the ending – which
Richardson's publishers pressured her to provide as the novels
continued to appear throughout the 1920s and 1930s – may be
read as a refusal of the still hegemonic closure devices of
marriage and death, as an attempt to keep her narrative options

open. Since it is always the ending which determines the significance of the whole, this deferral also motivates the reader to continue. Eleanor Dear's story, like that of Miriam's mother, contains both marriage and death, but the 'story' of Miriam Henderson contains neither. At the same time both (and neither) victim and adventuress, Miriam is a rewriting of the fictional heroine via 'the original contents of her mind. Her own images; what she sees and thinks.'

Hysteria, the semiotic and écriture féminine

Women generally write in order to tell their own family story (father, mother and/or their substitutes). When a woman novelist does not reproduce a real family of her own, she creates an imaginary story through which she constitutes an identity: narcissism is safe, the ego becomes eclipsed after freeing itself, purging itself of reminiscences. Freud's statement 'the hysteric suffers from reminiscence' sums up the large majority of novels produced by women.

In women's writing, language seems to be seen from a foreign land; is it seen from the point of view of an asymbolic, spastic body? Virginia Woolf describes suspended states, subtle sensations and, above all, colors – green, blue, – but she does not dissect language as Joyce does. Estranged from language, women are visionaries, dancers who suffer as they speak.

(Kristeva, 1974b: 166)

Pilgrimage, I would argue, offers one of the most sustained meditations on subjectivity within twentieth-century literature. It can be read as a protracted exercise in reminiscence, and indeed as a rewriting of Richardson's diaries;[4] either way it would qualify as one of Kristeva's 'hysterical' novels.

Kristeva's work on subjectivity, signifying practices and her concern with the significance of what was previously unsayable, is directly relevant to *Pilgrimage*. Her comment, cited above, is however open to a number of objections. Richardson's and Woolf's novels are as much *about* the constitution of identity, as they are attempts to constitute it, and *Pilgrimage* and *To the Lighthouse* are reminiscences which are also attempts, in Freud's phrase, at 'remembering, repeating and working through'. If one claims, on the other hand, that Richardson and Woolf (neither of whom 'reproduce a real family of their own') are *not* writing women's novels in Kristeva's sense, what would one then say they are writing? In addition, Kristeva's comment seems to ignore the point that Joyce or Lawrence may also create imaginary stories through which to constitute an identity, or may use writing as 'a place to shed one's sickness' in Lawrence's words. By this definition, could Joyce, Lawrence and Proust not also be called 'hysterics'?[5] In women's writing, she claims, language seems to be seen from a foreign land. Lawrence, Joyce and Proust have other reasons (class, colonialism, homosexuality) to motivate *their* estrangement from language, their treatment of language as a foreign land. And each, certainly, has problems with what Kristeva earlier in the same interview calls 'the phallic position' in language.

Kristeva takes a specific instance, the feminine, as a general symbol of forms of alienation produced by quite distinct and historically specific conditions. The naming of the subversive and dissident elements as 'feminine' (Kristeva in Marks and de Courtivron, 1981: 167) is an important political gesture, but one which is here undermined – quite disastrously I think – by her contrast between Joyce and Woolf. Woolf and, by implication, other women writers are allowed to be 'visionaries' and 'dancers', but it is Joyce who 'dissect[s] language'. The naming of the avant-garde as 'feminine' does not apparently disrupt the traditionally gendered opposition between the critical (dissection) and the creative (vision and dancing). But why, one might ask, should the presentation of subjectivity in *Pilgrimage* or *The Waves* be read as a colourful dance but that of, say, Molly Bloom in *Ulysses,* be read as a dissection of language? The distinction made here seems dubious, for in Lacanian (and Kristevan) terms every subject is, precisely, *subject* to language – not its master – and in this respect Joyce is in no better position to 'dissect' language than is Woolf. The image of the woman writer as the little mermaid indeed suggests the point that mermen too have tails, that they too must 'suffer as they speak'.

Defending the centrality of subjectivity in women's writing, Juliet Mitchell claims that 'it has to be the discourse of the hysteric. The woman novelist must be an hysteric' (1984: 289). Defining hysteria as the 'simultaneous acceptance and refusal of sexuality under patriarchal capitalism', she argues that by the very fact of *becoming* a writer, the woman novelist refuses the woman's world and that her construction of the world of women must take place 'from within a masculine world'. Kristeva's model depends on the Lacanian theory of women's negative entry into the symbolic, whereas Mitchell's argument also invokes the social ('patriarchal capitalism'). After defining the Lacanian notion of the symbolic as a point 'where sexuality is constructed as meaning', Mitchell takes issue with Kristeva's notion of a 'semiotic'. The semiotic, in Kristeva's work, is a preverbal moment when the child is still tied to the mother's body:

> At the same time instinctual and maternal, semiotic processes prepare the future speaker for entrance into meaning and signification (the symbolic). But the symbolic. . .constitutes itself only by breaking with this anteriority. . . . Language as symbolic function constitutes itself at the cost of repressing instinctual drive and continuous relation to the mother.[6]

While remaining 'inherent in the symbolic', the semiotic 'also [goes] beyond it and [threatens] its position'. In poetic language, or art generally, the irruption of the semiotic/maternal fractures or subverts the (paternal) symbolic order, thus producing 'this semiotization of the symbolic'.[7]

This notion of the semiotic, Mitchell argues, depends on a view of the oedipal and pre-oedipal as two separate structures, but if this is not the case, if on the contrary the oedipal is what defines the pre-oedipal (see the point on 'triangulation' in my previous chapter), then any semiotic disruptions of the law (or text) will take place within the terms of the symbolic. In an argument which clearly has implications for theories of *écriture féminine* as well as for Kristeva's *semiotic chora*, Mitchell concludes from this that,

> the only way you can challenge the church, challenge both the Oedipal and its pre-Oedipal, is from within *an alternative symbolic universe*. You cannot choose the imaginary, the semiotic, the carnival as an alternative to the law. It is set up by the law precisely as its own ludic space, its own area of imaginary alternative, but not as a symbolic alternative. So that, politically speaking, it is only the symbolic, a new symbolism, a new law, that can challenge the dominant law.[8]

Although the point about the impossibility of 'two structures' seems valid, it does not, it seems to me, necessarily invalidate Kristeva's 'semioticisation of the symbolic' – a concept which is immensely useful when reading Richardson and other texts – by men and women. The semiotic may be defined or 'set up by the law', as oppositional forces are always in some sense defined and 'set up' by the taboos and exclusions of the law, but its emergence, even within the terms of the symbolic, may offer a challenge. The challenge it offers may not 'politically speaking' *be* an alternative but in so far as it speaks of another world, another order of being, it represents *a vision of an alternative* – without which no change is possible.

Mitchell's last points would apply more to the theories of Luce Irigaray and Hélène Cixous than to Julia Kristeva. Believing neither in 'woman as such', nor in *écriture féminine*,[9] Kristeva has never posited the existence of a specifically female imaginary or a female symbolic. The symbolic function that she ascribes to women and women's writing is that of negativity – 'negative, in opposition to what exists, in order to say, "that's not it" and "that's still not it" '(1974 in Marks and de Courtivron, 1981: 137). This function, as I have argued in the previous chapters, is perfectly exhibited in *Pilgrimage*. In every move she makes, Miriam enacts this 'that's not it' – 'that's still not it', but she does more than this: her quest is also a search for a new symbolism, alternative modes of signifying the subject:

> There was a woman, not this thinking self who talked with men in their own language, but one whose words could be spoken only from the heart's knowledge, waiting to be born in her. (IV, 230)

In this respect *Pilgrimage* is closer to Hélène Cixous' project than to Kristeva's.

Against Kristeva's view of women as 'negativity', Cixous in 'The laugh of the Medusa' asserts women's affirmative role: 'We have no womanly reason to pledge allegiance to the negative. The feminine. . .affirms'.[10] Her well-known injunction to women to 'Write your self' stems from the conviction that an *écriture féminine* is both desirable and possible. A feminine writing, she argues, can be produced (by a man or a woman) which does not reflect 'woman' as the binary opposite of 'man', but which deconstructs that opposition and 'jams sociality'.

Cixous does not deny the difficulties of producing such writing, nor the power of the (patriarchal) symbolic order:

> Their 'symbolic' exists, it holds power – we, the sowers of disorder, know it only too well. But we are in no way obliged to deposit our lives in their banks of lack, to consider the constitution of the subject in terms of a drama manglingly restaged. . . .

As Morag Shiach points out,[11] the existence of the symbolic is conceded, although the term, by being placed in quotation marks, is problematised; while the phrase 'Their "symbolic"' implies the possibility of another, one which would be 'ours'. Like Richardson's woman 'whose words could be spoken only from the heart's knowledge' this would seem to imply an alternative language for women. According to Shiach's argument, the criticisms of Cixous' work as naïve or essentialist fail to take account of the extent to which she is talking about representations rather than the real – a point which could also be made about Richardson.

There are in fact a series of remarkable correspondences, theoretical and stylistic, between the text of *Pilgrimage* and Cixous' writing in 'The laugh of the Medusa' and *Newly Born Woman*: the critique of male definitions of woman; the aspiration towards a new and different language which will 'surpass the discourse that regulates the phallocentric system' (253); the presentation of bisexuality as two sexualities not a 'merger-type bisexuality' (254); the emphasis on women's plurality or 'the wonder of being several' (260) – even the reference to the myth of Perseus and the Medusa, which gives the Cixous essay its title, is present in *Pilgrimage,* though Miriam focuses not on the Medusa but on the plight of Andromeda: 'Because Perseus looked and rescued her, she would have to be grateful to him all her life and smile and be Mrs Perseus' (I, 459).

The same points, the same images occur within the same deliberate conflation of the lyrical with the philosophical. *Pilgrimage* seems like a perfect example of the practice of writing, which Cixous calls *écriture féminine* or which Luce Irigaray calls *le parler femme*: its unboundedness, fluidity, refusal of closure; its pleonastic, metonymic qualities; its orientation towards the concrete, the object, the quotidian; its use of ellipsis, syntactical inversion and its displacement of the sexual from the narrative to the textual level. All these are qualities claimed as characteristic of the writing described, and enacted, in 'The laugh of the Medusa'. Nevertheless, *Pilgrimage* cannot, in any simple sense, be read as an example of Cixous' and French feminist theories of *écriture féminine*.

It is, I would argue, not an example but *a precursor*,[12] an early attempt to theorise the possibilities of a women's writing which like 'The laugh of the Medusa' stages its own enactment of what those possibilities might consist of. This prescriptive/ enactive process produces, as with Cixous and Irigaray, problems of categorisation: *What* is being written? fiction or autobiography? poetry or theory? philosophy or something else? When genre boundaries are disturbed, the problem of how to read is inevitably posed, since reading depends on the series of signals provided within a given generic contract. One way of posing the problem of reading is to problematise existing reading habits, and this is of course what is common to both 'modernist' and feminist projects.

Another, somewhat different, problem emerges in the references to 'woman' and language. When Miriam claims that there is a woman waiting to be born in her, the implication is that this newly-born woman will have to find a new language in which to speak, that her birth *depends* on finding such a language. What she says at other points, however, seems to imply that this woman/voice is already in existence, but subordinate to the dominant masculine discourse:

> In speech with a man a woman is at a disadvantage – because they speak different languages. She may understand his. Hers he will never speak nor understand. In pity, or from other motives, she must therefore, stammeringly, speak his. He listens and is flattered and thinks he has her mental measure when he has not even touched the fringes of her consciousness. (II, 210)

On this question *Pilgrimage* slides between the actual and the possible, between the categories of woman as: (a) a male ideal/construction, (b) a historically situated speaker produced in relation to this construction; and (c) that which might escape/transcend existing definitions. It could of course be argued that this is a representation of Miriam's dilemmas, not of Richardson's views, except that in essays like 'Women and the future' the same slippages are evident:

For the womanly woman lives, all her life, in the deep current of eternity, an individual, self-centred. Because she is one with life, past, present, and future are together in her, unbroken. Because she thinks flowingly, with her feelings, she is relatively indifferent to the fashions of men, to the momentary arts, religions, philosophies, and sciences, valuing them only insofar as they are important in the evolution of the beloved.[13]

Richardson's 'womanly woman' here seems to be both a description of what is ('women'), and a recipe for what might be (the feminine) but it also comes perilously close to the masculine construction of the ideal ('Woman'). This is a key problem with Hélène Cixous, but not one confined to her – it seems to go with the territory of 'woman'. Jacqueline Rose, for example, makes a similar point about Kristeva:

Kristeva's work splits on a paradox, or rather a dilemma: the hideous moment when a theory arms itself with a concept of femininity as different, as something other to the culture as it is known, only to find itself face to face with, or even entrenched within, the most grotesque and fully cultural stereotypes of femininity itself.[14]

Thus it is not a question of using *Pilgrimage* as *evidence* of the theories of Kristeva, or Cixous or Irigaray, but of reading their different texts *as part of the same project*. Richardson's attempt to write 'her self', to write about 'femininity', led her as it did these later theorists into an inevitable engagement with the problems of representation and the real, the problem of the relation between subjectivity and signification.

One difference between Richardson's project and that of these later theorists, is that while these all, in different ways, explicitly engage with psychoanalysis, Richardson appears to ignore it. This cannot be explained as the difference between pre- and post-Freudian theorists of the feminine, for Richardson was familiar with psychoanalysis both through her friendships with Barbara Low (the psychoanalyst) and Bryher (analysed by Hanns Sachs). Her review of Low's *Psycho-analysis: A Brief Account of the Freudian Theory* in *The Dental Record* in 1920 establishes her early knowledge of psychoanalytic theories of sexuality and the subject. But with a few notable exceptions, *Pilgrimage* avoids any reference to the discourses of psychoanalysis.

The obvious explanation perhaps is that since Miriam

Henderson between 1891 and 1912 *was* pre-Freudian, any use of psychoanalysis would have constituted a betrayal of the principle of 'her own images, what she sees and thinks'. To present Miriam's development in psychoanalytic terms, as her contemporary May Sinclair does in *The Life and Death of Harriett Frean*, would be to position Miriam as the object of another's discourse, to produce a knowledge of her which would fix and stabilise her for the reader. Richardson's writing strategy, as I argued in Chapter 1, denies the reader this particular satisfaction; instead, it invites the reader to make her/his own interpretation of the material and to construct it according to their own theories and fantasies. This calls not only for the practical collaboration of the reader, but, potentially, for them to recognise the working of their own desires within the interpretive activity, in psychoanalytic terms to analyse the transferences they bring to their reading.

Whether or not one reads *Pilgrimage* as *écriture féminine*, it is, I think, an example of *écriture* which poses the question of the writing subject and of the relation between the subject who writes (*le sujet de l'énonce*) and the subject written about (*le sujet de l'énonciation*). What Richardson invites the reader to 'dissect', as much as Joyce does, but by other means, is the position of the subject in language.

Writing the subject

> The 'subject' of writing does not exist if we mean by that some sovereign solitude of the author. The subject of writing is a system of relations between strata: the Mystic Pad, the psyche, society, the world. Within that scene, on that stage, the punctual simplicity of the classical subject is not to be found.
>
> (Derrida, 1978: 226–7)

If *Pilgrimage* is a meditation upon subjectivity, it is also an extended reflection upon language and writing, in which the subject-matter (sexuality/subjectivity) can be read as an 'alibi' in the formalist sense, for an exploration of signification and the signifying process. In Richardson's writing it is difficult to tell the story from the discourse, since, as the Foreword recounts, the writing of a story becomes the story of a writing.

Writing here is many things: an attempt to subordinate the past to language, an attempt to get beyond language to net or enmesh some pre-verbal state or being, and an investigation of the question of the subject in language.

In her autobiographical sketches and other writings, Richardson often refers to herself in the third-person as 'one' or even as 'she' or 'D.R.' (1989: 113–14). In the Foreword to *Pilgrimage*, she alludes to herself only as 'the present writer. . . she', 'the author. . .she'. Using verbs in the passive form, making extensive use of present participles, there is a studied, often ingenious, avoidance of the pronoun 'I'. The 'Foreword', as Stephen Heath has pointed out, tells the story of writing *Pilgrimage* in a way which closely corresponds to Miriam's own decisions about writing described in *Dimple Hill*.[15] The problems of writing discussed in the 'Foreword' and the evasiveness about nominating the subject of writing as 'I' are thus illuminating for the text itself.

The novel-sequence dramatises the problem of how to use an 'I', how the subject uses a language which already speaks it, and which, in the case of a woman, inscribes her in a negative relation to the symbolic order. The alternation of third- and first-person ('she' and 'I') in effect draws attention to the position of Miriam as both the subject/object of discourse. Miriam is presented for the most part in the third-person, as 'she' by an unnamed, uncharacterised narrator. But within this narrative, sometimes within the same paragraph or sentence, an 'I' is allowed to appear. This shift is evident, for example, in the last paragraph of *Honeycomb* describing Miriam's reaction to an unspecified event – which we later learn is the suicide of her mother. I quote this passage at length to show the technique in action:

> The bony old woman held Miriam clasped closely in her arms. 'You must never, as long as you live, blame yourself, my gurl.' She went away. Miriam had not heard her come in. The pressure of her arms and her huge body came from far away. Miriam clasped her hands together. She could not feel them. Perhaps she had dreamed that the old woman had come in and said that. Everything was a dream; the world. I shall not have any life; all my days. There were cold tears running into her mouth. They had no salt. Cold water. They stopped. Moving her body with slow difficulty against the unsupporting air, she looked slowly about.

It was so difficult to move. Everything was airy and transparent. Her heavy hot light impalpable body was the only solid thing in the world, weighing tons; and like a lifeless feather. There was a tray of plates of fish and fruit on the table. She looked at it, heaving with sickness and looking at it. I am hungry. Sitting down near it she tried to pull the tray. It would not move. I must eat the food. Go on eating food, till the end of my life. Plates of food like these plates of food. . . . I am in eternity. . .where the worm dieth not and their fire is not quenched. (I, 489)

The passage starts in the third-person and ends in the first, but there are several first-person entries and unattributed sentences ('Everything was a dream') which might be either the narrator's or the character's. This is typical of Richardson's technique where there are frequently sentences or passages without any grammatical reference at all, observations which are unanchored to any stated subject-position.[16]

The subject's own discourse ('I am hungry' or 'I am in eternity') is positioned within a narrative passage in such a way that it presents the subject *at a specified moment*, not as a unified being existing throughout time, but at the moment of enunciation, using the present tense. The narrative discourse *about* the subject, generally in the past tense, is double-voiced because although it presents the scene in terms of Miriam, 'her own images' are never just her own; they are refracted via the narrator. The alternation of first- and third-person here, and in the text generally, has a number of effects: it may operate to intensify, to defamiliarise, or to interrupt the objectification. In each case, however, the grammatical shift affects the position of the reader. The uncertainty about who is speaking (narrator or character) unsettles the distinction between narrative (*histoire*) and discourse (*discours*). The problem of who is speaking also enacts the problem of what is happening at the narrative level.

At narrative level, one can trace two different 'stories' about the subject and subjectivity in *Pilgrimage*. In the first, signified in Miriam's name (her myr-iad 'I-ams') the subject is presented as multiple, bisexual, contradictory. The constant disavowal of any fixed subject position constitutes a deconstruction of the 'sovereign' subject, master of all it surveys. Like Kristeva's *sujet-en-procès* (subject-in-process or subject-on-trial), Richardson's subject seems always in the process of 'becoming', always an effect of time, place and relationships: 'I suppose I'm a new woman' (I, 436), 'I'm as much a man as a woman' (III, 221), 'I'm a Tory-Anarchist' (IV, 179); or, 'It's I who am your husband' (I, 456) and 'If anything I am my mother's son' (III, 220). This de-centred, deconstructive subject – 'Which self?' (IV, 318) – dominates the early part of the novel-sequence.

There is however, another quite different version of the subject in play, staged around the the question of 'being'. It is muted in the early chapters, but increasingly the possibility of a 'sense of identity, persistent, unchanging, personal identity' (IV, 304) becomes part of the story. It is as if *Pilgrimage* falls prey to a singular reversal: having set out, as it were, to demonstrate the myriad nature of the subject, it then becomes a quest to establish an 'essence' beyond those myriad subject-positions. What Miriam seeks is an ontological unity, a connection between her early childhood and her later 'selves'. An early memory, of being in a garden with the sound of bees humming, is used to represent the birth of consciousness. Composed of a series of sense impressions of the external world, the 'bee-moment' signals the existence of the subject as a separate being; it is repeated at different points throughout the novel-sequence. In the later novel-chapters, the desire for a more 'permanent self' is structured around the opposition between 'being' and 'becoming', and references to 'being' multiply in the last volumes.[17]

The opposition between 'becoming' and 'being', which is linked to a series of other oppositions between movement and stillness, action and contemplation, speech and silence, the future and the present, is also linked to Miriam's sense of sexual difference. Reflecting on the quality of Eleanor Dear's presence, Miriam claims women exist in the present in a way which she finds her male friends cannot:

> Men weave golden things; thought, science, art, religion, upon a black background. They never *are*. They only make or do; unconscious of the quality of life as it passes. (III, 280)

These oppositions are given fullest expression in Miriam's definition of herself against Hypo Wilson and it crystallises in her rejection of him – as man, as writer, as lover:

> Yet she knew that she would gladly sacrifice his companionship
> and all that depended therefrom for the certainty of seeing his
> world of ceaseless 'becoming' exchanged for one wherein should
> be included also the fact of 'being', the overwhelming, smiling
> hint, proof against all possible tests, provided by the mere existence
> of anything, anywhere. (IV, 361–2)

Her search for 'being' is related to her sense of 'becoming'
as a male preoccupation and it thus represents her search for
the 'real innermost civilisation of women', evident in the
passage cited earlier:

> Being versus becoming. Becoming versus being. Look after the
> being and the becoming will look after itself. Look after the
> becoming and the being will look after itself? Not so certain.
> Therefore it is certain that becoming depends on being. Man
> carries his bourne within himself and is there already, or he would
> not even know he exists. (IV, 362)

Miriam at this point resolves to nurture her 'being' and to
leave the becoming to take care of itself. But even as she
decides to opt for 'being', the feminine mode, the passage
textualises a 'masculine' drive for certainty, in the dogmatic
'Therefore it is certain'. In choosing 'being' over 'becoming'
Miriam becomes victim to the kind of oppositional logic which
elsewhere she is so critical of.

In *Clear Horizon* the desire 'to journey down to the centre
of her being' (IV, 347) is presented not as argument but
as experience, a mystical experience which liberates her,
momentarily, from the world of ceaseless becoming. Narrated
in the first chapter of the novel, the experience transports
Miriam 'beyond space and time' into a new sense of 'reality':

> With a single up-swinging movement, she was clear of earth and
> hanging, suspended and motionless, high in the sky, looking away
> to the right, into a far-off pearly-blue distance, that held her eyes,
> seeming to be in motion within itself: an intense crystalline
> vibration that seemed to be aware of being enchantedly observed
> and even to be amused and to be saying, 'Yes, this is my reality'.
> She was moving, or the sky about her was moving. Masses of
> pinnacled clouds rose between her and the clear distance, and just
> as she felt herself sinking, her spirit seemed to be up amongst
> their high rejoicing summits. (IV, 279)

Miriam's experience of 'being', as described here, seems not
a return to a single fixed 'I', but a dissolution of the 'I'. It is

a moment of ecstasy, a brush with 'eternity' in which individual identity is dissolved into a sense of being one with the external world. The passage links the experience to both religious and philosophical traditions and has a remarkable similarity to Plotinus' description of standing outside one's own body.[18] It also approximates to the 'oceanic' feeling described by Freud in *Civilisation and Its Discontents* as the basis of religious experience. Freud calls the religious impulse to transcend the boundedness of individuality 'oceanic', and quoting Grabbe, argues that 'We cannot fall out of this world...We are in it once and for all.'[19] For Miriam, her experience takes her both out of the world and self and paradoxically further into it:

> Whatever it was that had brought that adventuring forth (. . .) seemed at once the inmost essence of her being and yet was not herself; but something that through her, and in unaccustomed words, was addressing the self she knew, making her both speaker and listener, making her to herself, as strange and mysterious as, in the shaded lamplight, was the darkness behind the glowing fire. (IV, 281)

Freud compares the 'oceanic' experience with being in love, another case where the 'boundary between ego and object threatens to melt away' and links both to pathological states:

> There are cases in which parts of a person's own body, even portions of his own mental life – his perceptions, thoughts and feelings – appear alien to him and as not belonging to his ego; there are other cases in which he ascribes to the external world things that clearly originate in his own ego and ought to be acknowledged by it. (Freud, 1930/1961: 64–5)

As the text of *Pilgrimage* dramatises, there is a problem of how to read the experience. Writing it in a letter to Hypo, Miriam realises that he will read it as metaphorical:

> What she had just set down, he would take for metaphor. Up in the clouds. Seventh heaven. Any attempt to prove that it was not, would bring forth his utmost dreariness. He would light up (. . .) and say rather professorially that the prospect of having a child had given her a great emotional moment, was very much to her credit as showing her to be a properly constituted female, to be followed in due course by a return to the world of hard fact. (IV, 282)

In this passage Hypo's reaction is set up satirically via the stock phrases from his vocabulary: 'great emotional moment', 'properly constituted female', 'hard fact'. The reader is invited to judge the crassness of one who mistakes the literal for the metaphorical, who cannot *read* either language or woman. But since *this is the first time the reader is told of Miriam's prospective pregnancy*, the information disclosed here operates as a check. The reader is forced to reconsider in the light of the new information. Could it not be, after all, that the experience *does* link in some way to Miriam's new state of being? That pregnancy, like being in love, is another state in which the ego becomes uncertain of its own boundaries? Does Miriam's scorn of his 'professorial' diction conceal her own thought that there might be a connection? From Hypo's putative reaction, Miriam turns back to the problem of constatation: 'There were no words' (IV, 282). Her spiritual experience leads not away from, but back into the problems of language and meaning.

The problem of the literal and the metaphorical is returned to again (by Hypo) in the next chapter: 'when you said you had come down from the clouds, I thought you meant you were experiencing the normal human reaction after a great moment, not that you had been mistaken' (IV, 325).

What we learn here is that the phantom pregnancy is at an end, but also that the difference is not between the literal and the figurative, but between two different, equally metaphorical, readings of the same phrase. There can be no 'literal' account of her 'adventure in the sky' which is not open to different constructions, and, the text implies, there may strictly speaking be no 'literal' language at all. Miriam can no more escape the metaphorical than can Hypo, for as she later recognises 'We all live under a Metaphorocrasy' (IV, 607).

Unlike Proust, for whom metaphor was the instrument of poetic truth (Culler, 1982: 294), Richardson had reservations about metaphor as a trope. In her essay 'The rampant metaphor' for example, she writes: 'The thought-life of man if it is to maintain itself alive must go warily along a thread thrown forward across an abyss of metaphors'[20].

Like Nietzsche, Richardson distrusts the cognitive functions of metaphor, suggesting that it leads thought astray, especially where as in catachresis, the 'unknown' is rendered in terms of the 'known'. Catachresis, defined as the appropriation of an existing word to provide a name for something which does not have a name (e.g. 'a table leg', 'the foot of a mountain') is a way of naming the world in terms of what is already known. The disadvantages of this, for the woman writer, are clear.

Metaphor, imaged as one of the perils besetting any thinker, seems to stand for figurative language generally, but it may also be taken as a dislike of a trope based on similarity. The objection seems to be that metaphors propose/impose an equivalence between two things, whereas for Richardson there are multiple similarities and it is the role of the reader, in any given reading, to select from among these. According to this conception, metaphor is *more directive* than metonymy which, based on contiguity, allows a more oblique and plural chain of associations to arise.

Another objection to metaphor voiced by Richardson is that it reveals too much, too directly: 'By their metaphors ye shall know them' as she says in the same essay, or as Miriam states it in *Pilgrimage*, 'the metaphor you choose will represent you more accurately than any photograph' (IV, 331). Richardson, like Miriam, wants to avoid being pinned down, free to register 'the clamour of the way things state themselves from several points of view simultaneously' (III, 275). Her project to write the 'real inside civilisation of women' entails an avoidance of the traditional figure whereby the writer registers his/her perception of relations in the world as it is. If, as Julia Kristeva suggests, metaphor is linked to the 'paternal function' (1982: 53), Richardson's suspicion of it, and her preference for metonymic constructions may be seen not merely as an attempt to evade the *content* of most metaphorical constructions, but to circumvent the (masculine) habits of mind on which it is based.

Pilgrimage of course contains both metaphorical and metonymic figures and some figures which operate as both. In the 'bee-moment' for example, the memory is described in a series of contiguous sensations: the 'blazing' of the sunlight, the humming of the bees, the sight of sweet williams, etc., with a single simile 'smelling like hot paper' (I, 316). It is thus metonymic. But the meaning of the memory is none the less metaphorical; the subject's remembered sensations come to represent the birth of consciousness, 'the birthday of the world' (IV, 243). As a figure for renewal, its meaning can be transferred from one moment to another. Nevertheless, in so far as one can distinguish between metaphor and metonymy, it is metonymy – the linkage of signifiers in a relation of contiguity – which predominates. In particular, it is often via metonymy that the physical dimensions of the subject are registered.

Writing the body

> Write your self. Your body must be heard. (Cixous)

> 'the feminine [novels. . .are] too much set upon exploiting the sex motif as hitherto seen and depicted by men.[21]

In contrast to Joyce or Lawrence, Richardson is not noted for writing the body. The presentation of feminine consciousness in *Pilgrimage* seems to exclude areas concerned with the body, bodily functions, physical sensations. Unlike Molly Bloom, Miriam Henderson is not presented in mid-flow, making a row 'like the jersey lily'. Particular parts of the body remain unnamed, certain acts or experiences (urination, defecation, or orgasm) are not directly described. In *Pilgrimage* there is no Rabelaisian celebration of the 'low life' of the body to overturn the dominance of cultural codes. As one critic put it:

> There are whole areas of a woman's experience – every woman's experience – Miriam is not allowed to be conscious of. The bodily functions do not exist for her; in this respect, she is at one with the most conventional Victorian heroine of fiction. And the stream-of-consciousness technique makes us more aware of this. It is unfair, but next to impossible now not to think that Dorothy Richardson has cheated. (Allen, 1964: 38–9)

This comment is echoed in Showalter's that Richardson 'is afraid of the unique, the intimate and the physical' and Kaplan's that '"feminine consciousness" remains strangely abstract and separated from its normal connection with the body – which is the basic source of femininity'.[22] Richardson's text, despite its other similarities with Cixous' claims for *écriture féminine*, is found wanting in this respect.

As with Virginia Woolf, the absence of explicit reference to the body has been read as inhibition, 'prudishness' or a desire to challenge culturally established links between 'woman' and nature/the body. With *Pilgrimage*, one might argue that these omissions are part of the characterisation of Miriam Henderson, or that, as discussed in Chapter 4, the omissions are a way of staging the *non-relation* between the female body and feminine consciousness, of challenging the assumption of a unproblematic relation between the body and the subject. Femininity is situated in relation to the unconscious and language rather than the female body. One might also claim, as Rachel Blau DuPlessis does, that Richardson's sexual reticence, like her narrative pace and rhythm, constitutes a resistance to sexuality 'perceived only as arousal and climax' (1985: 151), but there are also the special problems of representing the female body for the woman writer in the early twentieth century. In painting, the female body has a genre all its own (the female nude) posing its own peculiar problems for the woman painter. For the woman writer of the nineteenth and early twentieth centuries, the set of literal and figurative terms for the female body presented, as Ellen Moers points out (1977: 254), a different but equally problematic heritage. Richardson's writing dramatises these difficulties in a very graphic way.

The body I would argue can be 'heard' in *Pilgrimage*, if one reads for it, if one listens 'differently' as Irigaray says. There are, contrary to Walter Allen's assertion, numerous references both to the body and bodily functions in the text. First of all there are the conventional visual images, generally of the face or head, by which Miriam's impressions of other characters are registered. Physical description is not assembled into neat descriptive paragraphs, but dispersed throughout the text, yet neither Miriam nor the other characters is disembodied. Miriam, for example, is called 'as fat as any German' by Mademoiselle (I, 174) and 'solid' by her mother (I, 198). Her consciousness of her own body is mainly referred to in scenes involving mirrors (I, 23 & 151) or when she imagines how her naked body would be seen by another (IV, 231). However, there is also, in the novel published in 1915, a passage when the subject remembers the onset of menstruation:

> She remembered with triumph a group of days of pain two years ago. She had forgotten. . . . Bewilderment and pain. . .her mother's constant presence. . .everything, the light everywhere, the leaves standing out along the tops of hedgerows as she drove with her mother, telling her of pain and she alone in the midst of it. . .for

> always. . .pride, long moments of deep pride . . . . Eve and Sarah
> congratulating her, Eve stupid and laughing. . .the new bearing of
> the servants. . .Lilly Belton's horrible talks fading away to nothing.
> (I, 137)

More obliquely, there is a reference to 'her body with its
load of well-known memories' (I, 263) which may be read, in
the context of a reflection on 'sins, past and present' as an
allusion to masturbation. Richardson's indirect method can be
seen in the passage following that reference:

> A sense of a checking of the tide that had seemed to flow through
> her finger-tips came. . .and Miriam knelt heavily on the hard floor,
> feeling the weight of her well-known body. The wallpaper attracted
> her attention and the honeycomb pattern of the thick fringed white
> counterpane. She shut the little book and rose from her knees.
> Moving quickly about the room, she turned at random to her
> washstand basin and vigorously rewashed her hands in its soapy
> water. The Englishman, she reflected as she wasted the soap, puts
> a dirty shirt on a clean body, and the Frenchman a clean shirt on
> a dirty body. (I, 263)

The passage moves from the sensations within the body (the
tide), to the body's relation with the external world (hard floor),
and thence metonymically to the detail of her surroundings
(wallpaper, counterpane). The ensuing actions, performed
'quickly' and 'vigorously', seem to indicate some decision has
been reached which the ritualistic cleansing action would seem
to confirm. The passage does not tell the reader how Miriam
has resolved her sense of sinfulness, whether the decision is
to renounce the practice, or the text which would proscribe it.
(The book she shuts is a 'preparation for Holy Communion'.)
But the reader's attention is attracted to 'the honeycomb pattern
of the thick fringed white counterpane', a tactile/visual image
which suggests the pleasures of touch, suggests perhaps the
texture of a woman's genitals and how these are 'fringed' with
pubic hair. This is a very different technique from the reference
to 'he had me always at myself 4 or 5 times a day sometimes'
(Joyce, 1922: 254), but it acknowledges the pains and pleasures
of the body in its own unique and intimate way.

Again, Miriam Henderson is not presented defecating
'Asquat on the cuckstool' as is Leopold Bloom, or urinating in
a chamber pot as is Molly Bloom in *Ulysses*, but she does go
to the lavatory. *Literally*; the euphemism is literalised. What is

described is not what she does there, but the room:

> The little lavatory with its long high window. . . .its little shabby
> open sink cupboard facing her with its dim unpolished taps and
> the battered enamel cans on its cracked and blistered wooden top,
> became this morning one of her own rooms. . . . (II, 217)

The reader has to infer the activities of the subject facing the
sink cupboard, just as s/he has to infer the body which sweats
from a reference to a 'musty' dress. There are clothes and there
are rooms; the body which inhabits them may have to be
inferred by the reader, and there is little of the *Hic est corpus
meum* found with Joyce's characters, but there is little reason
to doubt her corporeal existence.

One technique that Richardson does share with Joyce is
the way in which parts of the body are used as subject of
the action, so that *feet* go upstairs, *hands* light cigarettes. In
the 'normal' usage this would be written as 'She went
upstairs. . . she lit a cigarette'. The technique is similar to
Joyce's presentation of Leopold Bloom in *Ulysses* discussed by
Derek Attridge in *Peculiar Language*.[23] As Attridge points out,
the English language allows very little independence to organs
of the body; most verbs of conscious behaviour require a
grammatical subject (a name or pronoun), which tends to imply
an undivided, masterful and efficient self of which the organ
is a mere satellite or slave. What is perturbing in the examples
cited, is that the grammatical subject has ceased to be a human
subject, a part of the body seems to generate its own activity:
'The brown, tweed-covered arm of the little square figure
handed a tea-cup. The high, huskily hooting voice. . .' (II, 112).

This form of synecdoche (part for the whole) undermines,
momentarily, our belief in the human subject as unitary, as
capable of originating action from a single centre. It has other
effects too; the small linguistic variation, the substitution of
one signifier ('arm') for another ('Hypo/he'), gives the body a
new prominence. The body and its parts are not here subsumed
under the grammatical subject, but allowed a separate existence,
it becomes a *corps morcelé.*

The relation between the whole and the part is raised in
Dawn's Left Hand in a passage describing Miriam naked with
her lover. Her problem is to imagine her body as a whole,
since until now, only her face has been seen in public. She

sees herself as the object of three gazes, Amabel's, her own, and Hypo's:

> With the eyes of Amabel, and with her own eyes opened by Amabel, she saw the long honey-coloured ropes of hair framing the face that Amabel found beautiful in its 'Flemish Madonna' type, falling across her shoulders and along her body where the last foot of their length, red-gold, gleamed marvellously against the rose-tinted velvety gleaming of her flesh. Saw the lines and curves of her limbs, their balance and harmony. Impersonally beautiful and inspiring. To him each detail was 'pretty', and the whole an object of desire. (IV, 231)

Her appreciation of her body is mediated by the gaze of others, which is in turn constructed in relation to cultural icons of female beauty: the 'Flemish Madonna' and conceptions of what is 'pretty'. Both these standards are put into single quotation marks as if to isolate values which come from outside this scene. But her relation to the body is also mediated by the language used *without* quotation marks, in the Gerty McDowell phrasing of 'the rose-tinted velvety gleaming of her flesh' which recalls the euphemistic, soft-focus language of popular romantic fiction of the period. Once again, the point emerges that the subject's relation to her body can never be a direct 'natural' one, but is necessarily constructed within the cultural codes of her period.

The much-postponed consummation of her sexual relationship with Hypo Wilson is condensed into two brief paragraphs in the next chapter. Significantly, the two scenes are separated by a discussion of writing in which Miriam expresses her repudiation of male fiction ('Bang, bang, bang, on they go, these men's books, like an L.C.C. tram' (IV, 239)). The act of penetration is described as 'an instant's sudden descent into her clenched and rigid form' (IV, 257), and Miriam's physical sensations are presented figuratively, in terms of a journey through darkness towards the light:

> She was up at the high, glimmering window, saw clearly its painted woodwork and the small blemishes upon the pane against which she was pressed; through which, had it been open, she felt she could have escaped into the light that had called her thither. (IV, 257)

On this occasion, absorbed in the 'uncanny' (*sic*) nature of the journeying, Miriam does not make it through the pane into the light; her sexual initiation is non-orgasmic.

The description of sexual penetration as 'unwelcome' can be linked to another unwelcome instance of penetration, later in the same book-chapter, when Amabel in her 'determination to drive through veils and secrecies' (IV, 367) drops and breaks a casket containing Miriam's most treasured possessions. The incident has taken place earlier in the relationship between the two women, and the breakage is recalled and narrated only as their friendship itself begins to break up. The casket, which had belonged to her grandmother and contained her jewellery, is described as 'solid' with a double-lock; Miriam begins to consider whether the breaking had been accidental or whether 'it had been deliberately and forcibly flung down'. She reaches the conclusion that, 'Amabel was a tornado, sweeping oneself off one's feet and one's possessions from their niches' (IV, 367). The broken casket is used to symbolise Miriam's paranoia about being invaded as well as the invasive aspects of Amabel. However, given the equation between 'oneself' and 'one's possessions' between Miriam and the casket, it is also possible to read the casket incident, presented in detail and at some length, as a metaphor in another, more sexual, sense.[24]

Caskets and jewel-cases are symbols listed by Freud as means of representing female genitalia, along with all such objects enclosing a hollow space. However, according to Freud in the same essay, 'The complicated topography of the female genital parts makes one understand how it is that they are often represented as landscapes' (Freud, 1916/1961: 156). In *Pilgrimage* this landscape is usually a cityscape, a complex of streets, intersections, with churches, squares and houses rather than 'rocks, woods and water' mentioned by Freud. London 'this mighty lover' operates as a figure for the maternal body – as argued earlier – but also for the sexuality of the desiring subject. The erotic, desire and *jouissance* are textualised in the descriptions of Miriam's urban wanderings, her moments of blockage/stalemate as well as joy as she explores its riches. Thus her love for Michael Shatov transfers itself to,

> the changing same same song of the London traffic; the bliss of post-offices and railway stations, cabs going on and on toward unknown space.... (III, 86)

Desire spills out from her own body and from that of her object, on to the streets of London. It escapes elsewhere into the chain of discourse, metonymically.

The relation between desire and language is posed in its most complex and intimate form in Miriam's love-affair with Amabel. Their relationship begins with a written declaration of love and in a sense ends with a struggle over the written word – with Miriam's realisation that Amabel broke the casket to read her letters from Hypo. Hypo and Shatov are introduced gradually into the text, there is a slow narrative build-up to the relationships which follow, but the unnamed Amabel appears as 'a vision of the girl posed, her red gown glowing through the dark' and already, in the next line, 'the thought of her made a barrier beyond which nothing could pass' (IV, 185). Their relation is initially non-verbal, consisting of looks and sounds: 'a little trill' and 'a cooing, consoling deprecating laugh-sound' (IV, 188). From 'silent adoration' the girl moves quickly to physical contact:

> Her hands came forward, one before the other, outstretched, very gently approaching, and while Miriam read in the girl's eyes the reflection of her own motionless yielding, the hands moved apart and it was the lovely face that touched her first, suddenly and softly dropped upon her knees that now were gently clasped on either side by the small hands. (IV, 190)

The action, described with great precision, is in slow motion and attributed not to a named subject but to 'her hands' and 'the lovely face'. Once again the linguistic irregularities make 'normal' reading more difficult by delaying recognition and meaning-construction.

Amabel's declaration of love, again bypassing speech, is written on Miriam's mirror in 'lettering, large and twirly, thickly outlined as if made in chalk or moist putty'. '*I love you*,' it said' (IV, 196). The form of the writing here registers what Kristeva would call the semiotic within the symbolic. What Amabel offers the other woman (and seeks from her) is the mirroring gaze and words of love from the maternal relation. With the letter that follows this declaration, the contents are not conveyed, but its effect on Miriam is registered in the description of the writing it contains:

> A mass of small sheets, covered, without margins. Strange pattern
> of curves and straight strokes rapidly set down. Each separately.
> Gaps not only between each letter but also between the straight
> and the curved part of a single letter. Letters and words to be put
> together by the eye as it went along. (IV, 214)

Again the form (pattern, curves, strokes) is given all the
attention. *For Miriam as reader,* it is the visual effect of the
signifiers not their meanings which engages her. The signifiers
seem to function independently of the signifieds, and the
relation between the marks on the page and the gaps, between
the curved and straight components of individual letters
registered in minute detail. In one sense the technique here
is a kind of defamiliarisation, a close-up of the parts so that
the whole object (a letter), usually so familiar and mundane is
made strange. The passage offers in effect a minute analysis
of the process of reading, the ways in which the constituent
parts must be 'put together by the eye as it went along'. *For
the reader of Pilgrimage,* what this passage also signifies is the
extent of Miriam's attraction to Amabel, that the scrutiny of
the letter is a scrutiny of the body of the beloved.

The point is confirmed by Miriam's subsequent claim that
while letters written by men use the written word as a 'medium
of communication, recognizing its limitations and remaining
docile within them' (IV, 215), this letter from Amabel seems
to communicate the writer herself:

> Each word, each letter, was Amabel, was one of the many poses
> of her body, upright as a plant is upright, elegant as a decorative
> plant, supporting its embellishing curves just as the clean uprights
> of the letters supported the curves that belonged to them. (IV, 215)

In seeking the object of desire within signs themselves, Miriam
risks 'becoming lost in an unnecessary maze of sign reading',[25]
but it produces a discovery. What her desire impels her to
discover is a new way of imaging the body of woman, not *in*
language but *as* language, in the materiality of the signifier.

At the narrative level, the passage on writing in *Dawn's Left
Hand* marks a definite stage in Miriam's development as a
writer. Her interest in foreign languages and in *meanings* is
well documented in the earlier chapters, but here her interest
moves beyond the semantic, it becomes more technical as her
work as translator and reviewer increases. These linguistic

concerns are still geared to language as a social utterance: the differences between languages, the different uses to which men or women may put it, the relation between class and phonetic codes. What appear as (often lengthy) digressions on phonetics, chirography, or sociolinguistics can thus be seen not as digressive but as central to the story of a writer. Nevertheless, their status within the text is puzzling. Miriam's lecture to Hypo on the different pronunciations of the phrase 'How many irons are in the fire?' (IV, 161–6) *occupies six pages.* In reading it, it is difficult not to imagine a significance beyond the narrative or the characterisation of Miriam as a writer, and it seems, as Freud says, 'difficult to attribute too much sense to them'.[26]

Similarly, Miriam's reaction to a question in Amabel's letter seems excessive in both in terms of its strength and the amount of textual space allocated to it. The following is an excerpt from this passage:

> 'Isn't – E-g-y-p-t – a beautiful word?'
> *Beautiful?* If it were, she was tried in the balance and found wanting. Amabel stood turned away from her, posed in contemplation of something she could not see. . .
> Egypt. Neither the sound not the sight of the word was lovely. Written, with its three differently tailed letters properly joined, it was unmanageable: the tails competed. In the whole written language surely no word was more difficult to beautify. The opening sound uglier even than 'cheese', the pouting spit of the conclusion: hopeless. (IV, 216)

'Unmanageable. . .competed. . .uglier. . .hopeless'. Clearly these qualities do not apply to the referent (the country) but to something else. If, in the previous passage, the lines of letters and words stand for Amabel's (elegant) body, what kind of body, the reader might ask, does this word stand for? And why, if Amabel finds it 'beautiful' is Miriam 'tried in the balance and found wanting' and Amabel seem 'turned away from her'? *What could the word signify which would so divide the two women?* The passage appears trivial, digressive, about a minor difference in their attitude to a single word. And what's in a word, or as Richardson wrote as the title of one of her articles 'What's in a name?'. What appears to be in *this* name is its phallic 'tails'. The word displeases Miriam but not, she fears, Amabel, because it resembles the body of a man.

Miriam may recognise the 'Name-of-the-father' in the word from Amabel's letter, but beneath it she discerns the traces of an earlier structure. Her desire for the maternal, the pre-oedipal, breaks through and is recognised and she,

> acknowledged as she emerged from her reading, in herself and the girl, with them when they were together, somehow between them in the mysterious interplay of their two beings, the reality she had known for so long alone, brought out into life. (IV, 217)

Paradoxically, the reading of the letter takes Miriam beyond language, back to an archaic source of feeling which, once discovered, empowers the whole of her writing project. It is as if Amabel's 'effort to drive feeling through words', to express the love between them in writing, shows Miriam the way. Her earlier distrust of language has grown into a conviction that 'Words are separators, acknowledgement of separateness' (IV, 620), nevertheless it is *through* words that she feels she can gain access to 'the reality she had known so long alone' and it is through writing that Miriam will trace a pathway back to the source of her 'being', the mother.

In an earlier conversation with Michael, Miriam speaking of her mother claims:

> If there is a future life, all I care about is to meet *her*. If I could have her back for ten minutes I would gladly give the rest of my life. . . . (III, 220)

What does Miriam give the rest of her life to? To writing. Only in writing can she 'meet *her*', for the mother, like the body, is held in language. But as Cixous herself points out 'the mother too is a metaphor' (Cixous in Marks and de Courtivron, 1981: 252). It is only through language, the 'Metaphorocrasy' whose dominion Miriam once dreamed of escaping, that the subject (Miriam, Dorothy Richardson or her reader) can make her pilgrimage forward, and back, to what the text at different points calls 'reality' or 'life itself'.

Postscript

In my last chapter I read *Pilgrimage* primarily as a presentation of the subject, a study of the subjectivity of a woman over more than twenty years of her life. As such it is an extraordinary 'document' for no other writing from this period – fiction, history or case-study – offers such a detailed reading of a woman's life, of the mental processes of its single and singular subject. However, as I have argued, the text is not (just) a historical document, a presentation of a woman in a specific time and place, it is also an attempt to present a subject, a writer, able to reflect upon the discursive structures in which she is positioned. It is both a theory of the subject and a project to forge a new kind of subjectivity. Since the 'subject' is a central category in contemporary feminist debates, this attempt by an earlier twentieth-century feminist is of particular relevance for readers today. Richardson's decision to work on what Woolf called 'the damned egotistical self' may be a limitation in terms of 'Art' but in all other ways it is a gift.

The writing of *Pilgrimage*, to which Dorothy Richardson devoted most of her adult life, may be read as a form of self-analysis, a working-through of the divisions and contradictions within the writing subject. Perhaps all writing, whatever its project, is in some sense this. All such journeys are a *voyage autour de ma chambre*, meaning *de tout ce que je suis*, even in a *tour du monde*, as Miriam claims in the novel (IV, 167). For many of her contemporary novelists, the autobiographical project is concentrated into a single narrative, as in *Sons and*

Lovers, A Portrait of the Artist as a Young Man or *To the Lighthouse*. Richardson, however, took 'the journey down to the centre of being' as her major writing project. It may have had a therapeutic dimension as a 'writing cure' but for her, as for Freud, it had other justifications: 'discovery about oneself is impersonal, as well as personal, like a discovery in chemistry' (IV, 140).

In her discussion of *Pilgrimage* Elaine Showalter calls it 'the artistic equivalent of a screen, a way of hiding and containing and disarming the raw energy of a rampaging past' (1978: 262). She reads it as a defensive strategy, as obfuscation not discovery. Richardson also uses the word 'screen' not merely in the text but in her discussion of the collaborative reader:

> The process may go forward in the form of a conducted tour, the author leading, visible and audible, all the time. Or the material to be contemplated may be thrown upon a screen, the author out of sight and hearing, present, if we seek him, only in attitude toward reality. . . . (in Kunitz, 1933: 562)

Screen has a double meaning: that which conceals something and that where something is shown or revealed. *Pilgrimage* is a screen in this double sense, it conceals and reveals. The 'magic of the woven text' (III, 251) may hide certain issues in the way that Showalter suggests but it also allows one to see the ways in which the subject is a construction in language and to glimpse what has been discarded or repressed in order to make that construction. By gaps and silences, by using 'her own images; what she sees and thinks' (III, 285), the text lays bare the defensive device, just as in Freud's theory of the talking cure what is said (or not said) will reveal the patient.

With 'the author out of sight and hearing', the text-as-screen acts as a place for the reader to project his or her interpretive fantasies; as an intersubjective space where the vertical distinction between author and reader is blurred, in which positions interfuse leaving the stable subject (the 'author' or 'reader') disturbed, dissolved or out of focus. Interpretation, as the case of 'Dora' makes evident, always involves transference, the transfer of unconscious wishes or ideas by both the patient and the analyst (counter-transference). This recognition informs Richardson's writing strategy, her theory of the collaborative reader is based on an early recognition that all reading is transferential. If readers inevitably recreate the texts they read in their own image, the design of *Pilgrimage* forces them to look at that image, to recognise themselves and their activity among the faces on screen. It thus makes visible a number of problems about writing and reading, about who is doing what to whom in the complex business of reading and writing, in Wayne Booth's phrase. As I discussed in the last chapter, it also raises a number of questions for feminist theory and criticism.

My reading of the 'subject' in *Pilgrimage* draws, at times heavily, on the theoretical work of Julia Kristeva.[1] Both her emphasis on 'femininity' as a psychical position not reducible to biology and her theory of the semiotic and the symbolic as distinctive realms whose operations (and transgressions) are made visible in avant-garde writing are central to my argument. Kristeva developed many of these points in her early work on male writers (1974/1984), where she argues that irruptions of the semiotic, the maternal, in the work of male writers like Joyce, Lautreamont and Mallarmé is positive, pleasurable and revolutionary. When she does address women writers, Woolf and Tsvetayeva (and briefly Plath) in *About Chinese Women*, these semiotic irruptions are linked with danger and death rather than pleasure and progress. The suicides of these women writers are adduced as evidence of the dangers facing the woman writer who tries to represent the semiotic within the symbolic:

> Therefore the rush of these nonsensical, periphrastic, maternal rhythms in her speech, far from soothing her, making her laugh, destroys her symbolic armour: makes her ecstatic, nostalgic or mad. . . A woman has nothing to laugh about when the paternal order falls. (1977b: 30)

Male avant-garde writers standing on the barricades of the semiotic/symbolic are hailed as revolutionaries, whereas for the women writers involved in the same enterprise 'It generates voices, "madness", hallucinations' (1977b: 39). My point is not that the semiotic chora in these women's writings has (or should have) the same significance as in those of Joyce and others. If women have a different mode of entry into the symbolic, their relation to it, and to the semiotic, must clearly be different from that of men. Nevertheless, Kristeva's argument is problematic. It seems to suggest that for the woman writer the risks to the 'symbolic armour' are such that the revolution in poetic language is best left to the men or put off until another day: 'It is not certain that anyone here and now is capable of it' (1977b: 38). Yet Dorothy Richardson, like H.D., Mansfield, Colette, Rhys and numerous other women writers from this period whose writing is situated on the threshold did *not* commit suicide – although they had other problems which might be adduced to support the point. Kristeva's argument relies very heavily on her two examples, while with a larger or different set of examples, it might well be possible to show that there were (and are) alternative ways in which the avant-garde woman writer can write and survive.[2]

Similarly, Kristeva's category of the subject emphasises the internal differences *within* the subject rather than differences *between* subjects. At one level, this emphasis is very productive for the case of Dorothy Richardson and completely consistent with Kristeva's psychoanalytic project. At other points, however, it leaves the effects of changing historical conditions (in this period massive) either untheorised or generalised as 'Western, monotheistic capitalism' (1977b: 28). My emphasis on the social, on the historical relationships figured in the text is an attempt to argue that historically specific relationships *between* subjects are themselves constitutive of different forms of subjectivity. Wanting both to historicise the subject and to read it in terms of psychoanalytic theories (which are often either universalist or idealist or both) involves certain contradictions. The dilemma is another instance of looking both ways, 'feeling so identified with both, that I could not set either aside'. Miriam Henderson, who maintained that 'clear thought was incomplete thought' (IV, 362), would perhaps find this appropriate.

Despite my reservations and difficulties with Kristeva on her treatment of women's writing, on homosexuality, and the absence of any historical analysis of social relations in her concept of 'marginality',[3] I found her work on psychosexual development powerful and productive both in terms of the text and my understanding of the subject. Her later work on the maternal, on religious discourse and, increasingly, on the concept of love, has also played an important part in the ways

I have read these questions in *Pilgrimage*. This work is important because it brings together previously disparate areas – psychoanalysis, writing, politics – in ways which are vital for feminism.

One of the things the textual 'screen' of *Pilgrimage* made visible for me is another story of reading: my own history as a reader and the contradictions within this. Having started as 'a resisting reader' of male texts (Radford, 1975), I joined a feminist reading group to work on various theoretical texts by Macherey, Althusser, Lacan, Kristeva and others. My work in this group, the Marxist-Feminist Literature group described elsewhere by Cora Kaplan (1986: 61–4), lasted several years and was a formative experience. Then, after a certain amount of rereading the great tradition, my discovery of Richardson in the late 1970s moved me, rather belatedly, into the feminist rediscovery project. Fascination with the text, and the scarcity of friends and colleagues with whom I could discuss it, led in turn to my decision to write about it – to try to open it up in the ways described. But for the reader there can be no fresh start; at every point, traces of agendas set in the 1960s and 1970s, of reading habits and beliefs accumulated over the years, together with the shadows of my own doubts and uncertainties, rose up to meet me.

Ricoeur in *Freud and Philosophy* talks about two ways of reading; with suspicion and with faith. To read *Pilgrimage* I found I had to learn (and relearn) to read with faith as well as suspicion. To connect, to sustain a relationship with a long and complex text, working through disagreements and sometimes hostility, while recognising all the identifications and projections involved in such a relationship, is what reading *Pilgrimage* involved for me. Doing commentary on a text, as someone (Jane Gallop?) once said is like having an analysis. Richardson would have said that it was like 'life itself', for she uses reading as a metaphor for life. *Pilgrimage* is her attempt to create a new way of reading which might enable one to live in a different way, with all the intricacies of language and subjectivity, but without a master theory of either woman or writing.

Notes

Introduction

1. Dorothy L. Sayers, *The Unpleasantness at the Bellona Club* (1989), p. 197.
2. Elizabeth Wilson, in *Notebooks Memoirs Archives*, ed. Taylor (1982), pp. 61–2.
3. Fromm (1977), p. 394.
4. Leon Edel, *Modern Fiction Studies* 4 (Winter 1958), 1965–8.
5. Woolf, 'Romance of the heart', *Times Literary Supplement*, 19 May 1923, reprinted in Barrett (1979), p. 191.
6. Barthes (1977), p. 163.

Chapter One: Reading (in) Pilgrimage

1. Freud (1905/1960), pp. 36 and 117.
2. Koenigsberger and Mosse (1968), p. 11.
3. Richardson (1906) and (1939b).
4. MS Draft, 'Authors and readers', Yale Collection.
5. Richardson (1934), p. 94. See also Rose (1970) for a detailed discussion of Richardson's theory of reading.
6. See Beer (1983), pp. 213 ff.
7. Richardson's contemporary Frances Swiney argues this case in *The Cosmic Procession, or the Feminine Principle in Evolution*, cited in Showalter (1978), p. 186n.
8. This point was drawn to my attention by Jane Varley, Hatfield MA student.
9. Culler, 'Reading as a woman' in (1983), p. 54; Kamuf (1980), p. 286; Showalter (1979).

10. French (1982), pp. 4–5.
11. Docherty (1983), p. 239.
12. For Barthes' distinction between the 'writerly' and 'readerly' text, see Barthes (1975), p. 6.
13. Barthes, 'The reality effect', in Todorov (1982), pp. 11–17. All following quotations are from the text.
14. See Naomi Schor's *Reading in Detail* (1987), p. 97 for a brief discussion of the femininity of the detail.
15. See work by Davidoff and Hall, Davin, Dyhouse, Jeffreys, Lewis, Vicinus and Walkowitz.
16. Raymond Williams characterises the mcdernist project as 'taking nothing as it appeared but looking for deep forms, deep structures with the eyes of a stranger' (Williams, 1979: 223).
17. Hobsbawm (1987), p. 165.
18. See for example *Pilgrimage*, II, 30, 84, 96, 409–10; III, 204, 208, 277–9, 288.
19. Vicinus (1985), p. 5. See also Jeffreys (1985), chapter I.
20. George Egerton, 'Virgin soil', *Keynotes and Discords* (1983), p. 155.

Chapter Two: A form of quest

1. 'Led by her simpler mysticism, she gives her novel no structure whatsoever. She follows the stream-of-consciousness technique stolidly to its uttermost implications, and arrives at a simple, chronological sequence' (Kelly, 1954: 78).
2. Howard (1980), pp. 6–8.
3. See Greene (1951), pp. 93–5.
4. Bunyan's pilgrims 'solaced themselves for a season' in the Land of Beulah (1949), p. 216.
5. See Fussell (1980) and Dodd (1982), *passim*.
6. Beer (1983), p. 6.
7. *Line Upon Line*, 'by the author of the *Peep of Day*' was a Victorian manual of religious instruction for children.
8. See *Pilgrimage*, I, 27, 89, 298, 435; III, 333, 441.
9. Fromm (1977), p. 128.
10. Jones (1927), p. 56.
11. Bunyan, p. 151.
12. *Ibid.*, and Isaiah 62:4.
13. Jones (1927), pp. 37 and 40.
14. *Pilgrimage*, IV, 404–5, 433, 438, 440.
15. See Fromm (1977), pp. 367–71.
16. Roppen and Sommer (1964), p. 75.
17. Howard (1980), pp. 6–7.
18. Matthew 10:39.
19. Shirley Rose (1969), p. 375. See also the discussion on mysticism in Christ (1986), pp. 20–6.

20. For a brief discussion of being and becoming in the gospel of St John, see Frank Kermode: 'John' in Alter and Kermode (1987), pp. 452–3.
21. William James, cited in Christ (1986), pp. 20–1.
22. See Mackinnon (1978), p. 135.
23. Wendy M. Wright, 'The feminine dimension of contemplation' in Giles (1982), p. 105.

Chapter Three: London

1. Kristeva (1986), pp. 190–3. See also Sandra Kemp (1990) for an illuminating discussion of temporality in feminist modernist fiction.
2. Bakhtin (1981), p. 250. See also Bachelard (1957), p. 28.
3. Davis *et al.* (1982), pp. 306–7.
4. 'All my life, at least all my thinking life, I have been on a quest. My search has been with cne object in view, and that object has been to find myself.' (Kenney, 1924: 1) and for a similar statement (Pethick-Lawrence, 1938: 215).
5. Pankhurst (1914), pp. 6 and 12.
6. Pethick-Lawrence (1938), pp. 168–72. Jane Marcus's introduction to *Suffrage and the Pankhursts* (1986) argues on the other hand that, 'Sylvia's story *conflates* the personal with the political' (p. 5).
7. See Davidoff and Hall (1988).
8. Vicinus (1985), chapter 7. See also Robins (1907/1980).
9. Davidoff and Hall (1988), p. 358. See also Davidoff (1979), pp. 89–90.
10. Review of *The Tunnel*, *Times Literary Supplement*, 13 February 1919, reprinted in Woolf (1979), pp. 190–1.
11. Mansfield, review of *Interim* (1920/1987).
12. In the 1938 Foreword to the collected edition of *Pilgrimage*, Richardson quotes Goethe's Preface to *Wilhelm Meister*: 'The novel must proceed slowly, and the thought-processes of the principal figure must, by one device or another, hold up the development of the whole. . .' (I, 11).
13. See Walkowitz (1986).
14. The Savoy Hotel in 1889 was the first piece of rubber surfacing in the world according to Austin Coates, *The Commerce in Rubber* (Singapore and Oxford: Oxford University Press, 1987), photograph facing p. 145.
15. Bachelard (1957), p. 28.
16. Williams (1973), pp. 9–12.

Chapter Four: The enigma of woman

1. See Showalter (1978), chapter 7 *passim*.
2. George Egerton, 'A keynote to keynotes', in *Ten Contemporaries*,

ed. John Gawsworth (London: Joiner and Steele, 1932), p. 62.
3. Egerton, 'A cross line', in *Keynotes and Discords*, (London: Virago, 1983), p. 22.
4. Egerton, 'A cross line', p. 42.
5. Showalter (1978), pp. 248–62 and DuPlessis (1985), pp. 142–61. See Barrett and Radford (1978) which also argues that the third-person is a disguised form of first-person narration. There are of course good reasons for the feminist critic to make the connections between the life and the writing (see Todd, 1988).
6. 'Das Ewig-Weibliche', *Adelphi* (London, 1924), 1, part 4, pp. 364–6; 'I feel furious with the London Mercury. Arnold Bennett's letter tempts me to burst into epistolary vituperation and sue the reviewer for damaging libel. For it is damaging to say that because I have tried to convey the "fragmentary etc" world of an adolescent, therefore my view of life is fragmentary etc: abnormal and so on' (DR to Edward Garnett, 7 February 1920, University of Texas at Austin).
7. Fromm (1977), p. 153.
8. Joan Riviere, 'Womanliness as a masquerade' (1986). See also Stephen Heath's article 'Joan Riviere and the masquerade' in the same collection.
9. See analysis of this passage in 'What are men to Dorothy Richardson?', Fromm (1982).
10. Lacan, 'Guiding remarks for a congress on feminine sexuality', (1982), p. 90.
11. See for example Ouida's *The Moths* as an example of denunciations of 'feminine wiles' in popular fiction.
12. Cixous and Clément argue that the question 'What do women want?' conceals another more important one, that of women's pleasure (1986, p. 82).
13. See Jacobus (1986), p. 7.
14. Mendizabal employs the same code when he talks about Miriam to the Canadian doctors. He claims 'that he had only to lift a finger. . .' (II, 432), thus categorising her as a 'fille' and losing her the status of 'jeune fille' and an offer of marriage.
15. Jacqueline Rose, 'Introduction II', in Lacan (1982), p. 49.
16. 'All speaking subjects have within themselves a certain bisexuality which is precisely the possibility to explore all the sources of signification' (Kristeva in Marks and de Courtivron (1981), p. 165).

Chapter Five: Looking back

1. Felski (1989), pp. 135–6.
2. '*Pilgrimage*: the eternal autobiographical moment', in Fleishman (1983), pp. 452–3.
3. See Felski (1989), chapter 4.

4. Moretti (1987), pp. 18ff.
5. Marienne Hirsch, 'Spiritual Bildung', in Abel *et al.* (1983), p. 29.
6. Gloria Fromm, 'What are men to Dorothy Richardson?', *Women and Literature* 2 (1982), p. 172.
7. *Pilgrimage*, IV, 155–6.
8. See for example Chasseguet-Smirgel (1985), *Female Sexuality*, London: Carnac Books; Chodorow (1978); Irigaray (1985a) and (1985b); Kristeva (1977b) and (1980).
9. Freud (1933/1964), p. 129.
10. 'The discovery that she is castrated is a turning point in a girl's growth. Three possible lines of development start from it: one leads to inhibition or to neurosis, the second to change of character in the sense of a masculinity complex, the third, finally, to normal femininity' (*ibid.* p. 126).
    See also Rachel Bowlby, in Brennan (ed.) (1989), pp. 40–56 for a brilliant discussion of Freud's paper.
11. There is no reference to Havelock Ellis in *Pilgrimage* but Miriam's large 'Hands like umbrellas' (I, 56) are used to suggest a deviant element in her otherwise feminine physique, in the Ellis manner. See Radford (1986).
12. For further points on 'difference' see Radford (1989), pp. 32–3.
13. Freud (1933/1964), pp. 126–7: 'Her love was directed to her *phallic* mother; with the discovery that the mother is castrated...the motives for hostility, which have long been accumulating, gain the upper hand.'
14. Melanie Klein, 'Mourning and manic-depressive states', (1986), p. 151. See Klein's definition: 'persecution (by "bad" objects) and the characteristic defences against it, on the one hand, and pining for the loved ("good") object on the other, constitute the depressive position.'
15. Fromm argues (1982, p. 183) that 'Shatov does not arouse such powerful feelings as Wilson', whereas I would argue that it is partly because *Wilson* does not arouse such powerful erotic feeling that she can consummate her relation with him rather than Shatov.
16. See Beatrice Potter's and Virginia Woolf's diary entries on their attitudes to Jewish men which testify to the anti-Semitism of the period.
17. Weininger (1906), pp. 319–21. Weininger is mentioned in *Pilgrimage* (III, 482) and much of Miriam's discussion on individualism and Jewish women is drawn from his book.
18. Klein (1986), p. 153.
19. The model for Amabel, Veronica Leslie-Jones (Vera Grad) certainly experienced Richardson's encouragement of her marriage as a betrayal of their relationship. See her letters and an account of the relationship in Gillian Hanscombe (1982), pp. 172–3, and 178–80. See also Richardson's poem 'Barbara' in *Poetry* 27 November 1925.

20. Irigaray (1974), pp. 11–12.
21. Freud (1933/1964), p. 126.

Chapter Six: The subject of writing

1. See *Interim* (1919) where Mrs Bailey's reconstruction of Tansley Street 'was like a play' (II, 341); a man's admiration is 'part of a novel, true like a book' (II, 389), and another man's mind 'was a French novel' (II, 432).
2. DuPlessis (1985), pp. 142–61. These points are also discussed in Radford (1989), pp. 25–36.
3. Richardson, 'Literary essays, memory of 1909', cited in DuPlessis (1985), p. 150.
4. Fleishman (1983), p. 430.
5. Sigmund Freud, 'Some psychical consequences. . .', *SE* XIX (1925/1961), pp. 249–50.
6. Kristeva (1980), p. 136. According to Toril Moi the link between the semiotic and the feminine is inappropriate since 'no-one knows sexual difference in the pre-oedipal'. (Moi, 1985: 165). However, the problem of the *relation* of the symbolic and semiotic, as discussed by Mitchell, remains.
7. Kristeva (1974a, 1984), p. 79. See also Domna C. Stanton's helpful discussion of these issues in 'Difference on trial', in Miller (1986), pp. 165–7.
8. Mitchell (1984), p. 391. See also Stallybrass and White (1986), p. 201, for a similar critique of Kristeva.
9. Julia Kristeva, 'Women's time' (1986), pp. 187–211, pp. 13–35, and 'A partir de *Polylogue*' (1978).
10. Hélène Cixous, 'The laugh of the Medusa' in Marks and de Courtivron (1981), p. 255. The quotations which follow are from pp. 250–55 of this essay.
11. Shiach, 'Their "symbolic" exists' in Brennan (1989), p. 153.
12. Sandra Gilbert claims this for Woolf in the Introduction to Cixous and Clément (1986), p. xv.
13. 'Women and the future – a trembling of the veil before the eternal mystery of "La Gioconda"', *Vanity Fair* 22 (April 1924), 39–40.
14. 'Kristeva – take two', in Rose (1986), p. 157; and see Shiach, *op. cit.*, p. 156 on Cixous.
15. Heath (1983), pp. 131–2. He compares the passage in the Foreword with *Pilgrimage*, IV, 525.
16. See Ann Banfield, 'Describing the unobserved', in *The Linguistics of Writing* (1987), p. 273.
17. See *Pilgrimage*, IV, 298–9, 317, 337, 347, 362, 406–7, 409, 496.
18. 'Many times it has happened: Lifted out cf the body into myself; becoming external and self-encentred', Plotinus, *Enneads*, IV, 8.1 and V, 3.14, also cited in Russell (1962), p. 294.

19. Freud *SE*, XXI (1930/1961), pp. 64–5. In Kristevan terms, Miriam here moves out of the paternal realm of 'time and history' into the pre-verbal, pre-oedipal space associated with the maternal.
20. Draft essay, 'The rampant metaphor'. Cited in Hanscombe, D.Phil. thesis, p. 328, Bodleian Library, Oxford.
21. Richardson to Henry Savage, 6 January 1950, Beinecke Collection. Richardson's letter echoes Nietzsche's comment on truth as 'a mobile army of metaphors, metonymies, anthropomorphisms'.
22. Showalter (1978), p. 261; Kaplan (1975), p. 46.
23. Attridge (1988), pp. 160ff. My comments on Richardson are based on Attridge's analysis of this feature in Joyce's writing.
24. See Hanscombe (1982), and 'Dorothy Richardson's life-style of writing' in Hanscombe and Smyers (1987), p. 58. The text does, however, provide evidence that the nature of the desire is lesbian.
25. Freud *SE* XV (1916/1961), p. 156.
26. Freud *SE* II (1893/1955), p. 93n. See Mary Jacobus' use of this comment (1986), p. 229.

Postscript

1. I also found the very different formulations of Cixous and Irigaray (and Chodorow) offered useful ways of making connections with questions of the subject and language and have therefore made reference to these at various points. In a study of the present kind it was not possible to make a detailed comparison between these different theorists, but wherever possible I have indicated the relevant critiques, debates, etc. either within the text or in footnotes.
2. Kristeva does add, after the line cited above, that it might be 'A woman perhaps': 'It is not certain that anyone here and now is capable of it. An analyst conscious of history and politics? A politician tuned into the unconscious? A woman perhaps. . .' (1977b: 38).
3. See the critiques offered in Moi (1985), Mitchell (1984) and Rose (1986).

Selected bibliography

Works by Dorothy Richardson

Richardson, Dorothy (1915–38/1979), *Pilgrimage*. All page references to the 1979 edition, London: Virago.

(1989), *Journey To Paradise*, London: Virago.

(1906), 'Days with Walt Whitman', *Ye Crank* 4 (August 1906), 259–63.

(1907a), 'The odd man's remarks on socialism', *Ye Crank* 5 (January 1907), 30–3.

(1907b), 'Socialism and anarchy: an open letter to the "odd man"', *Ye Crank* 5 (February 1907), 89–91.

(1907c), 'Nietzsche', *The Open Road* I (November 1907), 243–8.

(1917), 'The reality of feminism', *The Ploughshare*, new series, (September 1917), 241–6.

(1920), 'Review of *Psycho-Analysis: a brief account of the Freudian Theory*, by Barbara Low', *Dental Record* XL (August 1920), 522–3.

(1922), 'Science and linguistics', *Dental Record* XLII (March 1922), 149–50.

(1924a), 'About punctuation', *Adelphi* I, part 11 (April 1924), 990–6.

(1924b), 'Women and the future – a trembling of the veil before the eternal mystery of "La Gioconda"', *Vanity Fair* 22 (April 1924), 39–40.

(1924c), 'What's in a name?', *Adelphi* II, part 7 (December 1924), 606–9.

(1925a), 'Women in the arts: some notes on the eternally conflicting demands of humanity and art', *Vanity Fair* 24 (May 1925), 47, 100.

(1925b), (as 'R. Theobald', pseudonym), 'Why words?', *Adelphi* III, part 3 (August 1925), 206–7.

(1928a), 'Das Ewig-Weibliche', *New Adelphi* I, part 4 (June 1928), 364–6.

(1928b), 'Mr. Clive Bell's Proust', *New Adelphi* II, part 2 (December 1928–February 1929), 160–2.

(1929), 'Leadership in marriage', *New Adelphi* II, part 4 (June–August 1929), 345–8.

146

(1930), *John Austen and the Inseparables*, London: William Jackson.

(1934), 'The artist and the world today, a symposium', ed. G. West, *The Bookman* 86 (May 1934).

(1939a), 'Yeats of Bloomsbury', *Life and Letters Today* 21 (April 1939), 60–6.

(1939b), 'Adventure for readers', *Life and Letters Today* 22 (July 1939), 45–52.

(1959), 'Data for a Spanish publisher', ed. Joseph Prescott, *London Magazine* 6 (June 1959), 14–19. Reprinted in *Journey to Paradise* (1989).

Studies of Dorothy Richardson

Barrett, Michele, and Radford, Jean (1979), 'Modernism in the 1930s: Dorothy Richardson and Virginia Woolf', in Francis Barker, Jay Bernstein, John Coombes, Peter Hulme, David Musselwhite and Jennifer Stone, (eds) *1936: The sociology of literature. Volume I – the politics of modernism*. Colchester: University of Essex.

DuPlessis, Rachel Blau (1985), 'Beyond the hard visible horizon', in *Writing Beyond the Ending: Narrative strategies of twentieth century women writers*. Bloomington: Indiana University Press, 142–61.

Edel, Leon (1958), 'Dorothy Richardson, 1882–1957', *Modern Fiction Studies* 4, 165–8.

[Fromm], Gloria Glikin (1963), 'Dorothy M. Richardson: the personal "Pilgrimage"', *Proceedings of the Modern Language Association* 78, 586–600.

[Fromm], Gloria Glikin (1964), 'Variations on a method', *James Joyce Quarterly* 2 (Fall 1964), 42–9.

Fromm, Gloria Glikin (1974), 'The misfortunes of Dorothy Richardson: a review essay', *Modernist Studies*, vol. 1, 59–64.

Fromm, Gloria Glikin (1976), 'Through the novelist's looking-glass', in Bernard Bergonzi, (ed.), *H. G. Wells: A collection of critical essays*, Englewood Cliffs, NJ: Prentice-Hall.

Fromm, Gloria Glikin (1977), *Dorothy Richardson, a Biography*, Urbana, Chicago, London: University of Illinois Press.

Fromm, Gloria Glikin (1982), 'What are men to Dorothy Richardson?', *Women and Literature* 2, 168–88.

Hanscombe, Gillian (1982), *The Art of Life: Dorothy Richardson and the development of feminist consciousness*. London: Peter Owen.

Powys, John Cowper (1931), *Dorothy M. Richardson*, London: Joiner and Steele.

Radford, Jean (1989), 'Coming to terms: Dorothy Richardson, modernism and women', *News from Nowhere* X (July 1989).

Rose, Shirley (1969), 'The unmoving center: consciousness in Dorothy Richardson's *Pilgrimage*', *Contemporary Literature* 10, 366–82.

Rose, Shirley (1970), 'Dorothy Richardson's theory of literature: the writer as pilgrim', *Criticism* 12 (Winter 1970), 20–37.

Rose, Shirley (1973), 'Dorothy Richardson: the first hundred years, a retrospective view', *Dalhousie Review* 53, 92–6.

Staley, Thomas (1976), *Dorothy Richardson*, Boston: Twayne Publishers.

Other relevant works

Abel, Elizabeth, Hirsch, Marianne and Langland, Elizabeth (eds) (1983), *The Voyage In: Fictions of female development*, Hanover: University Press of New England.

Adams, Parveen (1983), 'Mothering', *m/f* 8, 40–52.

Adams, Parveen and Brown, Beverley (1979), 'The feminine body and feminist politics', *m/f* 3, 35–50.

Allen, Walter (1964), *Tradition and Dream* London: Dent.

Alter, Robert and Kermode, Frank (eds) (1987), *The Literary Guide to the Bible*, London: Collins.

Attridge, Derek (1988), *Peculiar Language: Literature as difference from the Renaissance to James Joyce*, London: Methuen.

Bachelard, Gaston (1957), *Poétique de l'espace*, Paris: PUF.

Bakhtin, Mikhail M. (1981), *The Dialogic Imagination*, Austin: University of Texas Press.

Banfield, Ann (1987), 'Describing the unobserved', in Nigel Fabb, Derek Attridge, Alan Durant and Colin MacCabe (eds), *The Linguistics of Writing*, Manchester: Manchester University Press.

Barthes, Roland (1975), *S/Z*, London: Jonathan Cape.

Barthes, Roland (1977), *Image, Music, Text*, essays selected and translated by Stephen Heath, London: Fontana.

Barthes, Roland (1982), 'The reality effect', in T. Todorov (ed.), *French Literary Theory: A reader*, Cambridge: Cambridge University Press, 11–17.

Beer, Gillian (1983), *Darwin's Plots*, London, Boston, Melbourne and Henley: Routledge and Kegan Paul.

Brennan, Teresa (ed.) (1989), *Between Feminism and Psycho-analysis*, London: Routledge.

Brown, Dennis (forthcoming), *The Death of God.*

Bunyan, John (1678/1949), *Pilgrim's Progress.* All page references are to the World's Classics edition, London, New York, Toronto: Oxford University Press.

Caplan, Cora (1986), *Sea Changes, Culture and Feminism*, London: Verso.

Chodorow, Nancy (1978), *The Reproduction of Mothering*, Berkeley: University of California Press.

Christ, Carol P. (1986), *Diving Deep and Surfacing*, Boston, Mass.: Beacon Press.

Cixous, Hélène (1981), 'The laugh of the Medusa', in Marks E. and de Courtivron I. (eds), *New French Feminisms*, Hemel Hempstead: Harvester Wheatsheaf.

Cixous, Hélène and Clément, Cathérine (1986), *The Newly Born Woman*, Manchester: Manchester University Press.

Culler, Jonathan (1975), *Structuralist Poetics*, London: Routledge and Kegan Paul.

Culler, Jonathan (1982), *The Pursuit of Signs: Semiology, literature, deconstruction*, London: Routledge and Kegan Paul.

Culler, Jonathan (1983), *On Deconstruction*, London: Routledge and Kegan Paul.

Davidoff, Leonore (1979), 'The separation of home and work? Landladies and lodgers in nineteenth- and twentieth-century England', in Sandra Burman (ed.), *Fit Work for Women*, London: Croom Helm.

Davidoff, Leonore and Hall, Catherine (1988), 'My own fireside', chapter 8 of *Family Fortunes: Men and women of the English middle class 1780–1850*, Chicago: University of Chicago Press.

Davin, Anna (1978), 'Imperialism and motherhood' in *History Workshop Journal* 5, 9–65.

Davis, Tricia, Durham, Martin, Hall, Catherine, Langan, Mary and Sutton, David (1982), '"The public face of feminism": early twentieth-century writings on women's suffrage', in R. W. Johnson, G. McLennan, W. Schwarz and D. Sutton (eds), *Making Histories*, London: Hutchinson, 303–24.

de Man, Paul (1979), 'Semiology and Rhetoric', in *Allegories of Reading: Figural language in Rousseau, Nietzsche, Rilke and Proust*, New Haven, Conn.: Yale University Press.

Derrida, Jacques (1978), *Writing and Difference*, London: Routledge and Kegan Paul.

Derrida, Jacques (1979), *Spurs – Nietzsche's Styles*, Chicago and London: University of Chicago Press.

Docherty, Thomas (1983), *Reading (Absent) Character; Towards a theory of characterization in fiction*, Oxford: Oxford University Press.

Dodd, Philip (1982), *The Art of Travel: Essays on travel writing*, London: Cass.

Dyhouse, Carol (1981), *Girls Growing up in Late Victorian and Edwardian England*, London: Routledge and Kegan Paul.

Egerton, George (1983), *Keynotes and Discords*, London: Virago.

Felski, Rita (1989), *Beyond Feminist Aesthetics*, London: Hutchinson Radius.

Fleishman, Avrom (1983), *Figures of Autobiography*, Berkeley and London: University of California Press.

Flynn, Elizabeth A. and Schweickart, Patrocinio P. (eds) (1986), *Gender and Reading*, London: The Johns Hopkins University Press.

Fox, George (1694/1962), *The Journal*, London: J.M.Dent (Everyman).

French, Marilyn (1982), *The Book as World*, London: Abacus, Sphere.

Freud, Sigmund (1893/1955), *Studies on Hysteria* (with Josef Breuer), *Standard Edition*, vol. II, London: Hogarth Press.

Freud, Sigmund (1905/1960), *Jokes and their Relation to the Unconscious*, Translated as *Standard Edition*, vol. VIII, London: Hogarth Press.

Freud, Sigmund (1916/1961), *Introductory Lectures on Psycho-Analysis*, in *Standard Edition*, vol. XV, London: Hogarth Press.

Freud, Sigmund (1925/1961), 'Some psychical consequences of the anatomical distinction between the sexes', in *Standard Edition*, vol. XIX, London: Hogarth Press, 248–58.

Freud, Sigmund (1930/1961), 'Civilisation and its discontents', in *Standard Edition*, vol. XXI, London: Hogarth Press, 64–145.

Freud, Sigmund (1933/1964), 'Femininity', in *New Introductory Lectures on Psycho-Analysis, Standard Edition*, vol. XXII, London: Hogarth Press, 112–35.

Fussell, Paul (1980), *Abroad: British literary travelling between the wars*, Oxford: Oxford University Press.

Gérard Genette, (1972), 'Métonymie chez Proust', *Figures 3*, Paris: Seuil, 41–63.

Giles, Mary E. (1982), *The Feminist Mystic and Other Essays on Women and Spirituality*, New York: Crossroads.

Goethe, Johann Wolfgang von (1795–6), *Wilhelm Meister's Lehrjahre*, Berlin: Unger.

Greene, Graham (1951), *The Lost Childhood and Other Essays*, London: Eyre and Spottiswoode.

Grosz, Elizabeth (1989), *Sexual Subversions*, Sydney, Wellington, London, Boston: Allen and Unwin.

Hall, Radclyffe (1928), *The Well of Loneliness*, London: Jonathan Cape.

Hanscombe, Gillian and Smyers, Virginia L. (1987), *Writing for their Lives: The modernist women 1910–1940*, London: The Women's Press.

Heath, Stephen (1983), 'Writing for silence: Dorothy Richardson and the novel', in Susanne Kappeler and Norman Bryson (eds), *Teaching the Text*, London: Routledge and Kegan Paul.

Heath, Stephen (1986), 'Joan Riviere and the masquerade', in Victor Burgin, James Donald and Cora Kaplan (eds), *Formations of Fantasy*, London: Methuen, 45–61.

Hill, Christopher (1988), *A Turbulent, Seditious and Factious People, John Bunyan and His Church 1628–1688*, Oxford: Oxford University Press.

Hobsbawm, Eric (1987), *The Age of Empire*, London: Weidenfeld and Nicolson.

Howard, Donald (1980), *Writers and Pilgrims: medieval narratives and their posterity*, Berkeley: University of California Press.

Irigaray, Luce (1974), *Speculum: de l'autre femme*, Paris: Éditions de Minuit.

Irigaray, Luce (1985a), *Speculum of the Other Woman*, trans. Gillian Gill, Ithaca: Cornell University Press.

Irigaray, Luce (1985b), *This Sex Which Is Not One*, trans. Catherine Porter with Caroline Burke, Ithaca: Cornell University Press.

Jacobus, Mary (1986), *Reading Woman*, London: Methuen.

Jeffreys, Sheila (1985), *The Spinster and her Enemies: Feminism and Sexuality 1880–1930*, London: Pandora.

Jones, Rufus (1927), *The Faith and Practice of the Quakers*, London: Methuen.

Joyce, James (1922/1937), *Ulysses*, London: The Bodley Head.

Kamuf, Peggy (1980), 'Writing like a woman', in S. McConnell-Ginet, Ruth Barker and Nelly Furman (eds), *Women and Language in Literature and Society*, New York: Praeger.

Kaplan, Sydney Janet (1975), *Feminist Consciousness in the Modern British Novel*, London: University of Illinois Press.

Kelly, Robert Glyn (1954), 'The strange philosophy of Dorothy M. Richardson', *Pacific Spectator* 8, no. 1 (Winter 1954), 76–82.

Kemp, Sandra (1990), 'Feminism, fiction and modernism', *Critical Quarterly* 32, no. 1.

Kenney, Annie (1924), *Memories of a Militant*, London: Edward Arnold.

Klein, Melanie (1986), *The Selected Melanie Klein*, ed. Juliet Mitchell, Harmondsworth: Penguin Books.

Koenigsberger, H. G. and Mosse, G. L. (1968), *Europe in the 16th Century*, London: Longman.

Kristeva, Julia (1974a/1984), *Revolution in Poetic Language*, trans. Margaret Waller, ed. Leon Roudiez, New York and Guildford: Columbia University Press.

Kristeva, Julia (1974b), 'Oscillation du "pouvoir" au "refus"', in *Tel Quel*, Summer 1974, reprinted in Marks and de Courtivron (1981), trans. Marilyn A. August, *New French Feminisms*, Hemel Hempstead: Harvester Wheatsheaf.

Kristeva, Julia (1977a), *Polylogue*, Paris: Éditions du Seuil.

Kristeva, Julia (1977b), *About Chinese Women*, trans. Anita Barrows, London: Marion Boyars.

Kristeva, Julia (1978), 'A partir de *Polylogue*', interview with Françoise von Rossum-Guyon, *Revue des sciences humaines* 168 (December), 495–501.

Kristeva, Julia (1980), *Desire in Language: A semiotic approach to literature and art*, trans. Tom Gora, Alice Jardine and Leon Roudiez, ed. Leon Roudiez, Oxford: Blackwell.

Kristeva, Julia (1982), *Powers of Horror*, trans. Leon Roudiez, New York and Guildford: Columbia University Press.

Kristeva, Julia (1986), *The Kristeva Reader*, ed. Toril Moi, Oxford: Basil Blackwell.

Kunitz, S. J. (ed.) (1933), *Authors Today and Yesterday*, New York: Wilson.

Lacan, Jacques (ed. Juliet Mitchell and Jacqueline Rose) (1982), *Jacques Lacan and the École Freudienne: Feminine sexuality*, London: Macmillan.

Laplanche, J. and Pontalis, J.-B. (1973), *The Language of Psycho-analysis*, London: Hogarth Press.

Lewis, Jane (1984), *Women in England 1870–1950*, Hemel Hempstead: Harvester Wheatsheaf.

Light, Alison (1984), 'Returning to Manderley', *Feminist Review* 16, 7–25.

Mackenzie, Norman and Jeanne (1973), *The Time Traveller: The Life of H. G. Wells*, London: Weidenfeld and Nicolson.

Mackinnon, Donald M. (1978), 'Some epistemological reflections on mystical experience', in Steven T. Katz (ed.), *Mysticism and Philosophical Analysis*, London: Sheldon Press.

Mansfield, Katherine (1920/1987), 'Dragonflies' (review of *Interim*), in *Athenaeum*, 9 January 1920, reprinted in Clare Hanson (ed.), *The Critical Writings of Katherine Mansfield*, London: Macmillan, 64.

Marcus, Jane (ed.) (1986), *Suffrage and the Pankhursts*, London: Routledge and Kegan Paul.

Marks, Elaine and de Courtivron, Isabelle (eds) (1981), *New French Feminisms*, Hemel Hempstead: Harvester Wheatsheaf.

Masterman C. F. G. (1909), *The Condition of England*, London: Methuen.

Mayhew, Henry (1950), *London's Underworld*, ed. Peter Quennell, London: William Kimber.

Miller, Nancy K. (ed.) (1986), *The Poetics of Gender*, New York: Columbia University Press.

Minow-Pinkney, Makiko (1987), *Virginia Woolf and the Problem of the Subject: Feminist writing in the major novels*, Hemel Hempstead: Harvester Wheatsheaf.

Mitchell, Hannah (1968), *The Hard Way Up*, ed. Geoffrey Mitchell, London: Faber and Faber.

Mitchell, Juliet (1984), *Women: The longest revolution*, London: Virago.

Moers, Ellen (1977), *Literary Women*, London: W. H. Allen.

Moi, Toril (1985), *Sexual/Textual Politics*, London: Methuen.

Moretti, Franco (1987), *The Way of the World*, London: Verso.

Morrison, Toni (1983), 'Rootedness' in Mari Evans (ed.), *Black Women Writers*, Garden City, New York: Anchor Press/Doubleday.

Pankhurst, Emmeline (1914), *My Own Story*, London: Eveleigh Nash.

Pethick-Lawrence, Emmeline (1938), *My Part in a Changing World*, London: Victor Gollancz.

Radford, Jean (1975), *Norman Mailer: A critical study*, London: Macmillan.

Radford, Jean (ed.) (1986), *The Progress of Romance*, London: Routledge and Kegan Paul.

Ricoeur, Paul (1977), *Freud and Philosophy: An essay in interpretation*, New Haven, Conn.: Yale University Press.

Riviere, Joan (1986), 'Womanliness as masquerade', in Victor Burgin, James Donald and Cora Kaplan (eds), *Formations of Fantasy*, London: Methuen, 35–44.

Robins, Elizabeth (1907/1980), *The Convert*, London: The Women's Press.

Roppen, G. and Sommer, R. (1964), *Strangers and Pilgrims. An essay on the metaphor of journey*, Oslo: Norwegian University Press.

Rose, Jacqueline (1986), *Sexuality in the Field of Vision*, London: Verso.

Ruskin, John (1865), *Sesame and Lilies*, London: Smith, Elder.

Russell, Bertrand (1962), *A History of Western Philosophy*, new edition, London: Allen and Unwin.

Schor, Naomi (1987), *Reading in Detail: Aesthetics in the feminine*, New York and London: Methuen.

Showalter, Elaine (1978), *A Literature of Their Own: British women novelists from Brontë to Lessing*, London: Virago.

Showalter, Elaine (1979), 'Towards a feminist poetics', in M. Jacobus (ed.), *Women Writing and Writing about Women*, London: Croom Helm, 22–41.

Sinclair, May (1922/1980), *Life and Death of Harriett Frean*, London: Virago.

Stallybrass, Peter and White, Allon (1986), *The Politics and Poetics of Transgression*, London: Methuen.

Suleiman, Susan (1983), *Authoritarian Fictions: The ideological novel as literary genre*, New York: Columbia University Press.

Todd, Janet (1988), *Feminist Literary History: A defence*, Cambridge: Polity Press in association with Basil Blackwell.

Vicinus, Martha (1985), *Independent Women*, London: Virago.

Walkowitz, Judith (1980), *Prostitution and Victorian Society: Women, class and the state*, Cambridge: Cambridge University Press.

Walkowitz, Judith (1986), 'Science, feminism and romance: the men and women's club 1885–1889', *History Workshop Journal* 21 (Spring 1986).

Webb, Beatrice (1982), *The Diary of Beatrice Webb*, vol. I, ed. Norman and Jeanne Mackenzie, London: Virago.

Weininger, Otto (1906), *Sex and Character*, New York: Putnam's.

Williams, Raymond (1973), *The Country and the City*, London: Chatto and Windus.

Williams, Raymond (1979), *Writing in Society*, London: Verso.

Wolff, Janet (1985), 'The invisible *flâneuse*: women and the literature of modernity', in *Theory, Culture and Society* 2, no. 3.

Woolf, Virginia (1925), *The Common Reader*, London: Hogarth Press.

Woolf, Virgina (1929), *A Room of One's Own*, London: Hogarth Press.

Woolf, Virginia (1947), 'Street haunting', in *The Death of the Moth and Other Essays*, London: Hogarth Press.

Woolf, Virginia (1979), *Women and Writing*, ed. Michele Barrett, London: The Women's Press.

Index

Allen, Walter, 124, 125
Althusser, Louis, 138
anti-semitism, 98–9
Attridge, Derek, 127
Austen, Jane, 20

Bakhtin, Mikhail, 45–7
Barthes, Roland, 4, 11, 18–19
Bildungsroman, 29, 87
Boehme, Jacob, 41
Brontë, Charlotte, 56
Bryher, Winifred, 2, 115
Bunyan, John, 25, 26, 29, 30, 32, 35
  see also Pilgrim's Progress

Caird, Mona, 67
Canterbury Tales, 26
Carey, Rosa Nouchette, 9
Chodorow, Nancy, 86, 103
cinematic method, 26–7, 55
  see also Pilgrimage, method
Cixous, Hélène, 90, 112–15, 124, 133
Colette, 62, 137
Conrad, Joseph, 8–9, 20

Darwin, Charles, 29, 35
Derrida, Jacques, 66, 68, 105
detail *see Pilgrimage*
Doll's House, A, 49–50
DuPlessis, Rachel Blau, 68, 108, 125

écriture féminine, 3, 106–33
Edel, Leon, 2
Egerton, George, 22, 67–9
Eliot, George, 7, 56

Eliot, T. S., 3
Emerson, Ralph Waldo, 41
endings, 33, 108–9

Faraday, M., 35–6
father, 88–9, 91–7, 99
femininity, 70–4, 75, 78–9, 86, 92,
  100, 105, 106, 115, 124–5, 136
  see also gender identity, language,
  masquerade, mother, new
  woman, representation,
  sexuality, subject, symbolic
  order
Finnegans Wake, 7
Forster, E. M., 62
Fox, George, 34, 41
Freud, S., 6, 44, 105, 121, 129, 135

Geddes, Patrick, 10
gender identity, 80–3, 88, 91–2, 101
  see also femininity
Gibbs, Philip, 63
Gissing, G., 62
Goethe, Johann Wolfgang von
  see Wilhelm Meister
Grand, Sarah, 22, 67

H.D., 137
Heart of Darkness, 28
Heath, Stephen, 117
Hill, Christopher, 26
Hobsbawm, Eric, 20
Hungerford, Mrs (novelist), 9
Huxley, T.H., 9, 10, 35
hysteria, 109–11

Inferno, 30
interpretation, 135–6
Irigaray, Luce, 112, 113, 114, 115

James, Henry, 8, 11
  The Ambassadors, 11–12
James, William, 41
John, Gwen, 53
Joyce, James, 2, 3, 7, 13, 28, 29, 30,
  45, 58, 62, 108, 110, 116, 124,
  127, 136
  see also individual titles

Kaplan, Cora, 138
Kenney, Annie, 47
Kristeva, Julia, 45, 83–4, 91–2,
  109–12, 115, 118, 123, 130, 136–8
Künstlerroman, 8, 87

Lacan, Jacques, 76, 111, 138
language, 6, 11, 110–11, 113, 114,
  116, 117, 122, 125, 130, 132–3
Lautréamont, Comte de, 136
Lawrence, D.H., 110, 124
Lessing, Doris, 2
Low, Barbara, 115

Macherey, Pierre, 138
Mallarmé, Stephane, 136
Mansfield, Katherine, 51, 60, 66, 137
Marxist–Feminist Literature group,
  138
'masculinity complex', 92–3, 96, 105
masquerade, femininity and, 70–4,
  75–6, 78, 98, 101
Masterman, C. F. G., 62, 63
masturbation, 126
Maudsley, Dr Henry, 10
Mitchell, Hannah, 47, 48
Mitchell, Juliet, 110–12
modernism, 3
Moers, Ellen, 125
Morris, William, 62
Morrison, Toni, 16–17
mother, 82, 83–5, 86–105, 133
  see also femininity
mother/daughter relation, 88–9

narrative, 19, 118–19
new woman, 67–70, 75, 79–80
  see also femininity
Nietzsche, F., 66–7, 68, 82, 122

Odyssey, The, 33
Ouida, 8, 9

Pankhurst, Emmeline, 48
Passage to India, 28
Pethick-Lawrence, Emmeline, 47, 48
Pilgrim's Progress, 29, 30–4
  see also Bunyan, John
Pilgrimage
  see Richardson, Dorothy
Plath, Sylvia, 136
Plotinus, 121
*Portrait of the Artist as a Young Man,
  A*, 52, 135
Pound, Ezra, 3, 20
Powys, John Cowper, 45
Prelude, The, 87
prostitution, 21–4, 53–8, 98, 99
Proust, Marcel, 2, 8, 14, 110, 122
psychoanalysis, 115–16, 138
reader, collaborative, 4–5, 13–17, 47,
  58, 116, 123, 135–6
reading, as activity, 8, 11–12, 15,
  114, 131, 136
religion, 29, 30–1, 34–43, 66, 68,
  73–4, 77, 98, 121, 138
reminiscence, 109
representation, 70, 71, 74–8, 115
  see also femininity
Rhys, Jean, 62, 137
Richardson, Dorothy
  articles:
    'Data for a Spanish Publisher',
      7, 107–8
    'The Rampant Metaphor', 122
    'What's in a name?', 132
    'Women and the Future', 114–15
  books:
    Pilgrimage, 1–5
      bisexuality in, 113, 118
      body in, 124–30
      detail in, 17–19
      dreams in, 89–90, 95–6
      écriture féminine, 106–33
      gender identity in, 80, 84, 86,
        91–2
      as history, 19–21, 134, 137
      homosexuality in, 101–2
      as landscape, 129
      as meditation on subjectivity,
        109, 116
      metaphor and metonymy in,
        122–4
      method and technique of,
        3–5, 14, 16, 17–19, 24, 26–7,
        40–1, 50–5, 59–62, 69–70, 80,
        107–8, 116, 117–18, 127–8,
        131, 135–6

as a quest, 13–15, 25–43, 78,
    112
representation of women,
    77–8
as self-analysis, 133
Backwater, 8, 19, 30, 50, 69, 72, 73
Clear Horizon, 31, 37–9, 52, 61, 84,
    94, 98, 102–3, 120–22
Dawn's Left Hand, 31, 100–2, 106,
    127–31
Deadlock, 11, 19, 23, 30, 61, 94,
    97–8
Dimple Hill, 31–2, 39, 40–1, 117
Honeycomb, 15, 19, 30, 50, 72,
    78–81, 82–3, 93–6, 117–18
Interim, 23, 30, 53–8, 81–2, 97
March Moonlight, 4, 8, 28, 32–3,
    34, 39, 41–2, 60–1, 63, 69, 98,
    103–5
Oberland, 28, 31
Pointed Roofs, 7, 8, 15, 25, 26–7,
    29, 32, 34–5, 50, 71–2
Revolving Lights, 3, 16, 23–4, 30,
    84, 99
The Trap, 11, 30, 60
The Tunnel, 8, 10–11, 13, 18, 22–3,
    30, 41, 50–2, 57, 73–4, 77, 97, 106
short stories:
    'Summer', 80
Ricoeur, Paul, 138
Riviere, Joan, 72–3
Rose, Jacqueline, 115
Ruskin, John, 49

Sachs, Hanns, 115
'Sailing to Byzantium', 28
Sayers, Dorothy L., 1, 2
Schiller, J. C. F. von, 87
sexuality, 57, 85, 102, 116, 125
    see also femininity
Showalter, Elaine, 68, 124, 135

Sinclair, May, 116
social darwinism, 9–10
Sons and Lovers, 135
Spencer, Herbert, 10, 35
Stanton, Elizabeth Cady, 43
subject, subjectivity, 109, 110, 115,
    116–24, 133, 134, 137
    see also femininity
symbolic order, 111–13, 117, 136, 137
    see also femininity

Tolstoy, L. N., 11
Trilling, Lionel, 4
Tsvetayeva, Marina, 136

Ulysses, 13–14, 28, 126–7

Vicinus, Martha, 21, 49

Webb, Beatrice, 44, 48
Weininger, Otto, 66, 99–100
Well of Loneliness, The, 92
Wells, H. G., 39, 47, 63
Whitman, W., 7
Wilde, Oscar, 2, 19, 75
Wilhelm Meister, 34, 87, 88
Williams, Raymond, 62, 63
women's suffrage, 47–8, 66
Woolf, Virginia, 3, 14, 20, 51, 57, 66,
    83, 107, 124, 134, 136
    A Room of One's Own, 57, 64,
        78–9, 83
    'Modern Fiction', 108
    'Mr Bennett and Mrs Brown', 107
    Mrs Dalloway, 58, 62
    Night and Day, 58
    Orlando, 83
    'Street Haunting', 58–60
    To the Lighthouse, 28, 109, 135
    The Voyage Out, 28
    The Waves, 110